If God Is Your Co-Pilot, Swap Seats!

James W. Moore

CHRISTIAN LARGE PRINT
A part of Gale, Cengage Learning

GALE
CENGAGE Learning·

Detroit • New York • San Francisco • New Haven, Conn • Waterville, Maine • London

LIBRARY OF CONGRESS CATALOGING-IN-PUBLICATION DATA

Moore, James W. (James Wendell), 1938–
    If God is your co-pilot, swap seats! / by James W Moore.
        p. cm.
    ISBN-13: 978-1-59415-311-2 (softcover : alk. paper)
    ISBN-10: 1-59415-311-6 (softcover : alk. paper)
    1. Christian life. 2. Large type books. I. Title.
    BV4501.3.M6635 2009b
    248.4—dc22   2009040099

Published in 2009 by arrangement with Riggins International Rights
Services Inc.

10-359
(GALE)
CHRISTIAN
2 | 10
17.99

Printed in the United States of America
2 3 4 5 6   14 13 12 11 10

ED034

*To June in celebration of our fifty great
years together and her five-year
milestone*

CONTENTS

INTRODUCTION

Not long ago, I saw a bumper sticker that read "If God Is Your Co-Pilot, Swap Seats!" That tongue-in-cheek message is simply reminding us that it is so important to get our priorities right. It is so crucial to know how (with the help of God) to put first things first, to choose God as the number one priority in our lives, to love God because God first loves us.

I had a speech teacher in college who liked to say, "Don't put the em-PHA-sis on the wrong syl-LA-ble!" What she meant, of course, was to be sure in speaking that you put the emphasis on the right syllable. The same holds true in life. We need to be sure (always with the help of God and by the grace of God) to emphasize the right things, to put the emphasis where it belongs: on God; to put God and the doing of his will first in our lives.

I do like that bumper sticker, because I

think its message (which I will say more about in chapter 1) is something we all need to hear and to be reminded of constantly, namely this: don't just take God along for the ride. Rather, let God do the driving, invite God to be the driving force in your life. Put God in the driver's seat. Don't make him your assistant driver whom you just call on every now and then when the going gets rough and the road is treacherous. Ask him (and really mean it) to be the chief pilot in your life's journey. Recognize him as the number one *priority* in your life every single day. Don't think of him just as a backup plan when trouble comes.

Remember that classic scene in Shakespeare's play *The Tempest.* The mariners realize that a dangerous storm is approaching. They are terrified. They try everything they know to try and then in despair they cry, "All lost! to prayers, to prayers! all lost!" Sadly and unfortunately, that scene pretty well describes how some people relate to God. They just ignore God until trouble rears its head and then they want to pull God out like a last-resort rabbit's foot to save them from whatever problem they may be facing at the moment and then after God does indeed save them, they are perfectly content to nudge God back off the stage into the shadowy wings, so they can take center stage again. But God wants to be so much more to us than that.

The great Christian Augustine once put it perfectly when he said, "Our hearts are restless till they find rest in Thee." This is how we are wired. This is how we are made. We can't be content or satisfied apart from God. So the message is clear: put God first! Turn the driving over to God! Choose God and the doing of his will as your number one priority. Invite God to take over the driver's seat in your life!

CHAPTER ONE:
IF GOD IS YOUR CO-PILOT, SWAP SEATS!

SCRIPTURE: MATTHEW 6:25–33

Let me tell you about something I like to do when I'm driving. When I see a bumper sticker I like to pull up next to the car to see if the message on the bumper sticker fits the driver. Sometimes it clearly does. For example, I saw a bumper sticker the other day that said, "Don't Worry, Be Happy!" I pulled alongside the car, and saw that a young woman was driving the car. She was smiling, singing along with the loud music on the radio, bobbing her head and shoulders to the beat of the music, and tapping out the rhythm on the steering wheel. She was not worrying; she was being happy.

And then I saw one this week that read, "God Bless John Wayne." I pulled up to see a guy wearing a cowboy hat. He was so into the John Wayne syndrome that when we stopped at a traffic light, I fully expected him to roll down his window, point at me, and say, "Listen up and listen good, pilgrim!"

But then, on the other hand, sometimes the driver and the bumper sticker message just don't seem to go together at all. For instance, recently I saw a very profane, off-color bumper sticker on a very nice and expensive car. I pulled up alongside and was amazed to see that the driver was a lady, probably in her late eighties. It makes you wonder what's happening to our world.

A few weeks ago, I saw a car with a bumper sticker on it that said, "Honk if You Love Jesus." So I pulled up alongside and honked and smiled and waved. The driver looked at me angrily and acknowledged my honk with a gesture that I don't think was a Christian sign! In all my study of church history, I don't recall that particular gesture ever being listed in any age as a sign and symbol of the Christian faith. That gesture and that message just don't go together. There is something wrong with that picture. So you never know whether or not the bumper sticker message really reflects the lifestyle of the driver.

However, I saw a new message the other day that I really like. It said, "If God Is Your Co-Pilot, Swap Seats." I never could catch up with that car to see if the driver fit the message or not. But I do like that message. Now, what I think that means is something we all need to hear, namely this: don't just take God along for the ride. Rather, let him do the driving! Put God in the driver's seat of your life. Don't make him your assistant. Let him be the chief pilot in your life's journey.

Some months ago, I pulled into a service station to get some gas. I met a young man there who recognized me. He told me that he really enjoyed our church on television. I invited him to come join us, that we would welcome him with open arms. He responded by saying he is not ready just yet to make that kind of commitment. He said he was still "enjoying life" and having a great time sowing his wild oats. He indicated that he did believe in God and that maybe he would come and get involved in the church someday when he got older, but then he added, "To tell you the truth, Jim, what I'm really hoping for is one of those neat deathbed conversions!"

In his own way, he was saying, "God can be my co-pilot, but I really don't want to put him in the driver's seat . . . at least not yet because I'm having too much fun."

Unfortunately, there are many people around today who think like that. They

15

think of God as one who frowns on our fun, slaps our hands and says, "Naughty, naughty. Mustn't do!" They think of Christianity as something old, negative, and prohibitive. For these people, religion does not give life; it takes life away, and they could not be more wrong!

What a gross misunderstanding of the Christian faith that is! We need to always remember that Christianity is good news! That's what the word *gospel* means — "good news," "glad tidings."

God is not only a comfort, he is a joy. He is the source of all pleasure. He is light and laughter. He is the Giver of Life — real life, abundant life, full life, meaningful life, joyful life, eternal life. And our chief purpose is to celebrate him, and serve him, and enjoy him forever.

That's what our text for today in Matthew 6:33 is all about. Let me translate it like this: "Seek first the kingdom of God, and his righteousness, and everything else will fall in place for you."

Remember that scene from Disney's version of *Alice in Wonderland* in which a lock with legs is running around in a panic? Frantically, the lock runs here, there, and yon. Finally, Alice says to the lock, "What are you doing? Why are you running around in all directions?" And the lock says, "I am seeking the key to unlock myself!"

Well, that is precisely what Jesus is giving us here in Matthew 6. He says: "Here it is! Here is the key that will unlock you. You don't have to run around in a panic all the time. Here is the key to life. Just celebrate God as the King of your life and the Lord of all your relationships. Let that be your number one priority. Put that first, then everything else will fall into place for you and your life will be full of joy and zest and purpose and mission and meaning and ful-fillment."

Now, let me break this down a bit and bring it closer to home with three thoughts.

THE FIRST KEY TO LIFE IS TO SEEK GOD'S WILL

We can pray to God about anything. We can talk to God about our joys and sorrows, our victories and defeats, our blessings and our complaints, but the bottom-line prayer for the Christian is "Thy will, O God, be done."

Have you heard about the man who de-cided to write a book on the great churches of America? He decided to take a long trip across the country visiting the churches firsthand. He started in California. He was looking around and making photographs of

17

this church in San Francisco when he noticed a golden telephone on a wall. Underneath the phone was a sign that read, "$10,000 per minute." Intrigued, he found the church's minister and asked about the golden phone. The minister said, "Oh, that's a direct line to heaven and if you want to use it, you can talk directly to God." "Thank you very much," the man said, and he continued on his way. As he traveled across the country, he found the same golden phone with the same sign in Nevada, Arizona, Colorado, Illinois, Nebraska, and New York. At each site, he made the same inquiry about the golden phone and got the same answer.

Finally he arrived in Texas and behold! He saw the same golden telephone with a sign. But this time the sign read, "Free Calls." Fascinated, he found the minister and said, "Pastor, I've been all across the nation, and in many churches I found a golden telephone like that on the wall there. And in each state, I was told it was a direct line to heaven and that I could use it and speak directly to God for $10,000 a minute. But here your sign reads, 'Free Calls.' Why is that?" The pastor smiled and said, "Simple, my son. You are in Texas now . . . and it's a local call from here!"

Now, that story is a little Texas humor. But the real truth is: it's a local call anywhere. Wherever we are, we have a direct line to heaven. Wherever we are, God is available and accessible. Wherever we are, it's a free local call! And we need to make lots of those calls seeking God's will for our lives.

We had a delightful member of our church who prayed to God constantly. She was ninety-eight years young, and prayer was as natural to her as breathing. Like Tevye in *Fiddler on the Roof* she just talked to God about everything. Once she said this to me: "Well, Jim, when it comes to prayer, here's how I do it: I just say, 'Now Lord, here's what I want,' then I tell him, 'I want this, I want that, and the other,' and then I say, 'but, O Lord, have it your way 'cause you're a lot smarter than I am.' " This was just her down-home way of saying "thy will be done."

And she was so right. God is so much smarter than we are. God can see the big picture so much better than we can. So the key to life is, first of all, to seek God's will — and follow it.

The Second Key to Life Is to Obey God's Word

As the old-timers used to say: "It's in the Book!" The key to life, the key to happiness, the key to morality, the key to ethics, the key to fulfillment can be found in the Bible, in the pages of Scripture. That's why the Bible is so important for us. It's our survival kit, our instruction manual, and our blueprint for building the kind of life God wants us to build. It has the answers we long for and the solutions we so desperately need to make life work. But our problem is that sometimes we are not sure we want God in the driver's seat. So we neglect the teachings of Scripture. We either fail to trust what the Bible teaches, or worse, we choose not to do what the Scriptures command.

Some years ago, a television program preceding the Winter Olympics featured some blind skiers being trained to do slalom skiing, impossible as that sounds. Each blind skier was paired up with a sighted skier. The blind skiers were taught on the flats how to make left and right turns by following one command of their sighted skiing partners. When that was mastered, they would go up to the slalom slope where their sighted partners skied beside them shouting instructions at the appropriate moments:

"Left!" . . . "Right!" . . . "Straight!" As they obeyed the commands, they were amazingly able to negotiate the difficult course and cross the finish line, depending solely on the sighted skiers' word. It was either complete trust or complete catastrophe.

That is a great parable for the Christian life. In this world we are often blind about what course to take, which way to turn. We must rely on the word of the only One who is truly sighted: God himself. To avoid catastrophe, we follow his commands. His word gives us the direction we need to finish the course. So if you are wondering about something — "Should I do this or not?" — look at the Ten Commandments! If what you are contemplating violates any one of the Ten Commandments, then don't do it.

So if you are trying to make a decision — "Should I do this, that, or the other?" — look at Jesus, look at what he taught, look at what he stood for! If you cannot do what you are contemplating in the spirit of love, in the spirit of Jesus, then *don't do it!*

There is a wonderful true story about an American professor who traveled to London some years ago to do some postdoctorate study. While there, he attended the University Church of Christ the King in London.

21

Sunday after Sunday as he worshiped, he was touched deeply by the beauty of the music. Not only the singing of the choir but also the singing of the congregation, especially from a cluster of people who sat near him in the back of the church.

One Sunday, he asked the minister who those people were. The minister told him that they were the cast of *Godspell* that was playing in London at the time. He said that many of those young people had had no acquaintance with the Christian faith before they got into the cast of *Godspell*. But now, night after night, they sang the words from the gospel, the words of *Godspell*. He said the words began working on them. And so they sought a place and a people who cared about those words, believed those words, followed those words, lived those words, and they found that place and those people there at the church.

The point is clear: once you get the words, once you understand what is being said in the gospel, the godspell, then you want to be a part of it. You want to share it and live it and sing it. So the key to life is to seek God's will and to obey God's word.

THE FINAL KEY TO LIFE IS TO LIVE GOD'S WAY

Leo Buscaglia told a wonderful story about a student he had at the University of Southern California (USC) some years ago. The student's name was Joel, and Joel was absolutely miserable. Joel felt useless and worthless and joyless. He was depressed. One day Joel told his professor, Buscaglia, how unhappy and how unfulfilled he was. In despair, Joel said, "There is not one thing in my life that is worthwhile." Buscaglia said, "Okay Joel, let's go make a visit." Buscaglia took Joel over to the convalescent hospital near the campus at USC. Inside there were many older people, lying on beds, staring at the ceiling. As they walked into that scene, Joel looked around and said, "What am I doing here? I don't know anything about gerontology." Buscaglia said, "Good. You see that lady over there on the bed? Go over and say hello to her."

"That's all?" Joel asked.

"Yes, just go over there and say hello."

So Joel went over to the woman and said hello. She looked at him suspiciously and asked, "Are you a relative?" Joel said, "No." And she said, "Good. Sit down."

So Joel sat down and they started to talk. Buscaglia wrote: "My goodness, the things

23

she told him. She told him all kinds of things about love, about pain, about suffering, and even about approaching death and dying . . . with which she had made her own peace. She knew all these things, but nobody cared to listen to her" (except now Joel).

Well, Joel started going to visit once a week. It was so regular that in the hospital they named that day "Joel's Day." Buscaglia said that the greatest day in his teaching career was when he was walking across the campus one Saturday afternoon, and there was Joel, like a pied piper, with thirty older people stretched out behind him. He was taking them to the coliseum to see a football game.

Somewhere in heaven God was smiling because that's God's way — to find your life, your joy, your meaning, and your mission by reaching out in love to help other people.

Jesus put it like this: "Whoever will lose himself will find himself." The key to life is to seek God's will, to obey God's word, and to live God's way to make God the number one priority in your life!

CHAPTER TWO:
THE PRIORITY OF
GOD

SCRIPTURE: ACTS 2:1–4

Some years ago, there was a man who grew up in a mill town. He had wanted to go to college, but he came from a modest home and when he finished high school there was no money available for college, so he took a job at the mill.

This man and his wife had a son. He was an only child, and the man was determined to send his son to college. He wanted his son to have a better life and he knew the answer was college. So the day his son was born, the man placed a pickle jar on the floor beside the dresser in the master bedroom. Each night when he got ready for bed, the dad would empty his pockets and toss his coins into the jar. He did this every night for years and years.

When the jar was filled, the dad would sit at the kitchen table and roll the coins before taking them to the bank. Taking the coins to the bank was a big production, and when his son grew a little older he always got to go along with his dad on the trip to the bank. "These coins are going to send you to college someday," the father would say to his young son. "I want you to have a career. It's too late for me, but these coins are going to help you have a better life."

Each time as the dad slid the box of rolled coins across the bank counter toward the cashier, the dad would grin proudly and he would say, "These are for my son's college fund. I didn't get to go to college myself, but my son is going when the time comes. I'll see to that." Then father and son would celebrate at the ice-cream parlor. The son always got chocolate and Dad always got vanilla. When the clerk at the ice-cream parlor handed the dad his change, the dad would show his son the few coins nestled in his palm. "When we get home, we'll start filling the jar again," Dad would always say.

The dad always let his son drop the first coins into the empty jar. As they rattled around with a brief happy jingle, the father and son would grin at each other. "You'll get to college on pennies, nickels, dimes, and quarters," Dad would say. "But you'll get there. I promise you that."

The years passed and the son did go to college. He did well, graduated, and took a fine job in another town. Once while visiting his parents, he went into the master bedroom to make a phone call and noticed that the pickle jar was gone. It had served its purpose and had been removed. A lump rose in the son's throat and he stared at the spot beside the dresser where the jar had always stood. His dad was a man of few words, but through that pickle jar, the dad had taught his son the values of determination, perseverance, faith, and sacrificial love more eloquently than words could ever express.

A few years later, the son married a lovely woman named Susan, and he told her the story of the pickle jar and how it defined more than anything else how much his dad loved him. He told his wife that no matter how rough times were (even the summer when his dad was laid off from work for several months), not once would his dad take a single dime from that pickle jar. He would take on odd jobs to pay the bills but he would not touch the money in that pickle jar.

Some time later, the young son and Susan had a baby girl. They named her Jessica. The first Christmas after Jessica was born, they spent the holidays with the son's parents. After dinner, his mom and dad sat next to each other on the couch in the den and took turns holding and cuddling their first grandchild. Jessica began to whimper softly, so Susan took her from their arms and said, "She probably needs to be changed." She carried baby Jessica back to the master bedroom to change her diaper. When Susan came back into the den there was a strange mist in her eyes. She handed Jessica back to Granddad. She then took her husband's hand and led him back into the room. "Look," she said softly, her eyes staring directly toward a spot on the floor beside the dresser. To her husband's amazement, there (as if it had never been removed), stood the old pickle jar, the bottom already covered with coins.

The son walked over to the pickle jar, dug down in his pocket, and pulled out a fistful of coins. With a gamut of emotion choking him, he dropped the coins into the jar. Just then, he heard a noise behind him. He turned to see that his dad had walked into the master bedroom. His dad was smiling. His dad was holding baby Jessica. He had provided for his son. Now, he would provide for the one who followed his son.

Now, what does this story have to do with you and me? Actually, quite a lot because the story reminds us that God the Father (through sacrificial love) gave his Son the strength he needed — and he doesn't stop there. He also gives all those who follow the Son the strength, the help, the encouragement, and the support they need. This is the good news of our Christian faith: the Holy Spirit of God comes to give us strength and power, wherever and whenever we need it.

The great writer Mark Twain is, of course, most famous for his classic novels *Tom Sawyer* and *Huckleberry Finn.* However, in the late 1800s, he was also known as a popular lecturer as well as the author of several travel books. He got his start in the travel book area when he journeyed into the American West and as far as Hawaii. He then published informative and humorous articles about his trips, first in Western newspapers, and then national newspapers.

At the time when travel was slow, laborious, and difficult, Mark Twain was often away from home for long periods of time and his friends often did not know where to get in touch with him. One particular evening, a group of his friends realized his birthday was approaching. They wanted to send a birthday greeting, but they had no idea where he was, so they prepared a birthday letter; they all signed it, and then addressed it to:

Mark Twain
God Knows Where

A few weeks later, they got a response from Twain. He sent a note with just two words: "He did."

This is the good news. God knows where we are and what we need. He comes to us wherever we are to give us the help and power we need in that given moment. Let me show you what I mean with three thoughts.

FIRST OF ALL, IT IS GOD WHO EMPOWERS US TO FORGIVE

God knows where and when we need to forgive, and he sends the Holy Spirit to enable us to forgive. If we got in a time machine and went back to the day of Pentecost and said to Simon Peter, "Wow! What you did today was absolutely amazing. After what they did to Jesus you stood there and preached forgiveness with astonishing courage and conviction and grace. And your sermon was so powerful that 3,000 people came forward to join the church. How did you do that?" Peter would say, "It wasn't me. It was the power of the Holy Spirit."

If someone has done you wrong, and you are trying to find the strength to forgive all by yourself, all on you own, you are not going to be able to do it. It is the Holy Spirit that empowers us to forgive. When someone hurts us, we want vengeance! We want to get 'em back! We want to fight and show them a thing or two! That's our preferred reaction until we open our hearts to God. It is God who enables us to forgive, or better put, when we forgive, it's not really us, it is the gracious Holy Spirit of God forgiving through us. Let me illustrate that.

Lewis Grizzard died some years ago and I miss him and his homespun humor. In his books and newspaper columns, he often wrote about growing up in Georgia. One of my favorites was his column in which he reminisces about growing up in a little Methodist church and how it was so dear to his childhood. His church was small and had to share its preacher with another congregation and on Sunday nights had MYF: Methodist Youth Fellowship. When two brothers in town broke into a store, they were punished by being sent to MYF for six months.

The first night they were there, they beat up two fifth graders and threw a Cokesbury hymnal at the lady who met with us and always brought cookies. She ducked just in time and then looked squarely in their devilish eyes. Then soft as the angel she was, she said, "I don't approve of what you boys did here tonight . . . and neither does Jesus. But if He can forgive you, I guess I'll have to." She handed them a plate of cookies.

Lewis Grizzard concluded his column with these words:

And the last I heard, both those boys grew up and they're daddies now with steady jobs . . . and they rarely miss a Sunday at church. That was the first miracle I ever saw.

It was the miracle of forgiveness. Now, if we could find that MYF leader today and say to her, "How did you do that? How did you put up with those rowdy boys?" You know what she would say? She'd say, "Wasn't me. Left to my own devices, I would've poured the Kool-Aid on their heads and called the sheriff. But the spirit of Jesus was in me. It was the Holy Spirit within me that gave me the strength to forgive."

When we find the grace to forgive, it is simply because we are being carried by the presence and power of the Holy Spirit.

Don't miss this: if you are unable to forgive, if you are having great difficulty forgiving someone who has hurt you or disappointed you, it may be a spiritual red flag. It may mean that you have drifted away from the spirit of God. That's number one. The Holy Spirit enables us to forgive.

SECOND, IT IS GOD WHO EMPOWERS US TO LOVE UNCONDITIONALLY

It's easy to love those who are attractive to us. It's easy to love those who love us back. But unconditional love? Now that's something else. Love to all freely given, love expecting nothing in return, love with no strings attached, love even to those who hurt us. Only God's Holy Spirit can give us the strength to love like that; only God's Holy Spirit can enable us to love like Jesus loved. Let me show you what I mean.

In the early 1980s, a young man from Lancaster County, Pennsylvania, went to Colombia to fulfill his lifelong dream. He had a mission heart and all of his life he had prepared himself to go to Colombia so he could translate the Bible into the native language there and share the good news of the Scriptures with those people. But in January of 1981, this young man, Chet Bitterman, was kidnapped by Colombian rebels. They beat him, shot and killed him, and left his body in a hijacked bus. Imagine how his parents and loved ones back in Pennsylvania must have felt because of the senseless and brutal death of this fine, innocent young man.

A year later, following the leadership of Bitterman's parents, the churches and civic groups in Lancaster County, Pennsylvania, decided to do a demonstration of international Christian goodwill. They raised money to buy an ambulance and then they gave the ambulance to the state of Meta in Colombia, the place where young Bitterman had been killed.

Bitterman's parents traveled to Colombia for the ceremony. They made the presentation of the ambulance. After the ceremony, a reporter asked the parents, "How could you do this? How could you reach out in love to these people after what happened to your son here?" Bitterman's mother said, "We came in love because we are Christians. We serve Him who said, 'They'll know you are Christians by your love.' We are able to do this because God has taken the hatred from our hearts."

When we are able to forgive, and when we are able to love unconditionally, it's because the Holy Spirit is within us.

THIRD, IT IS GOD WHO EMPOWERS US TO BUILD A CHURCH

Only the Holy Spirit of God can build a church. Only the Holy Spirit can empower the church. Only the Holy Spirit can sustain the church. A church without the Holy Spirit is no church at all.

Have you seen the hit movie *Mr. Holland's Opus*? It's wonderful. It's the story of a dedicated music teacher named Glenn Holland. At the beginning of his career, Mr. Holland dreams of becoming a famous composer. He dreams of living in Hollywood and writing theme songs for movies, but he never gets to do that. Instead, he spends his entire career working with young students at John F. Kennedy High School.

With great tenderness, he works with a red-haired girl with pigtails who wants to play the clarinet, but no one believes in her. No one helps her; no one encourages her but Mr. Holland. With great compassion, he works with an African American student who wants to play the drums, but has a terrible time finding the beat. With great patience, he works with a street-wise tough kid who has a lousy attitude and is down on the world. And Mr. Holland helps them all and hundreds more like them.

The conclusion of the film is a classic. Mr. Holland retires, and as he cleans out his music room at the high school, he tells his wife and his son that he feels like such a failure. He never accomplished his great dream; he never went to Hollywood; he never became a famous composer. With slumped shoulders, he heads out of the school, but then he hears a noise in the auditorium. He opens the door and sees that the auditorium is jam-packed with his former students. They give him a long, thunderous, standing ovation. They have come back to express their love and appreciation to this wonderful man who gave so much of his life to them.

Then, the little girl with the red pigtails goes to the microphone. She's all grown up now and, in fact, she is the governor of the state. She says, "Mr. Holland, we know that you never got to become the famous composer you dreamed of being, but don't you see? Your greatest composition is what you did with us, your students. Mr. Holland, look around you. We are your great opus! Mr. Holland, we are the music of your life!"

Our calling as a church is to be God's music to the world, to sing the song of forgiveness, to sing the song of love, to sing the song of the church's great faith. But we can't do that alone, and the good news of the Christian faith, the good news of Pentecost, is that we don't have to do it alone. God is with us. God is our strength, our guide, our provider, our inspiration, our comfort, our teacher. The Holy Spirit empowers us and enables us to forgive, to love unconditionally, and to build the church. And that's why God should do the driving, that's why God should be in the driver's seat, that's why God should be the number one priority in our lives.

Chapter Three:
The Priority of
God's Three Ways
of Acting

SCRIPTURE: MATTHEW
28:16–20

Recently, I read about some high school sophomores who were asked by their English teacher to write a definition of love. The teacher said some of the answers were not so much definitions as they were "daffynitions." For example, one student wrote: "Love is the feeling in your stomach . . . of butterflies wearing roller skates."

Another said, "Life is one thing after another! Love is two things after each other."

But here is my favorite. A student wrote these profound words: "Love is the feeling you feel when you feel you are going to have a feeling like you have never felt before."

Now that's a definition, isn't it? The point is that love is terribly difficult to define. Something that powerful and wonderful defies description. Words aren't big enough. It is so deep, so amazing, so awesome that it's just hard to put it into words. It's hard to define love, but we have all experienced it, haven't we?

The same thing is true with some of our basic Christian beliefs. Take, for example, the doctrine of the Trinity. It's hard to define, but we can experience it! Let me ask you something. If I passed out pencils and paper right now, and asked each one of you to write your definition of the Trinity, what would you put down? The truth is that most of us would have difficulty because this belief of "One God in Three Persons" is very confusing to many people. Let me show you what I mean.

Some years ago Cardinal Richard Cushing was walking through Macy's department store in New York City. The manager of the store recognized the noted and famous Catholic priest and ran up to him saying, "Cardinal Cushing, thank God you are here! Come quickly! A man has passed out over here. He may have had a heart attack! He may be dying!"

Let me hurry to say that the man had only fainted, and in a matter of minutes he would be perfectly OK, but Cardinal Cushing, not knowing that, rushed over to the collapsed man as any good priest would do, knelt beside him, took his hand tenderly, and began to administer the last rites. Cardinal Cushing said to the man, "My friend, do you believe in God the Father, God the Son, and God the Holy Spirit?" The man roused a little, opened one eye, looked at the people standing around, pointed to Cardinal Cushing, and said, "Can you believe this guy? Here I am dying and he asks me a riddle!"

Well, for many people, the doctrine of the Trinity is indeed a riddle: Father — Son — Holy Spirit? One plus one plus one equals one? One God in Three Persons? It does sound confusing and complex. What does it mean? And how does it affect your life and mine? Let me give you the key that helps unlock this theological puzzle, the key that pushes back the heavy door of this belief, and lets us inside so we can understand it better and celebrate it more. Here it is: the key is to remember that every doctrine was first a doxology, every belief was first a song! This means that we come to this belief, not looking for what is here to argue about, but rather looking for what is here to sing about; not looking for what is here to squabble over, but instead looking for what is here that makes us want to shout and sing praises to God.

The doctrine of the Trinity is like the concept of love. We don't have to worry about defining it; rather we just experience it! We relish it, feel it, celebrate it! Well, what is here to sing about? When we start at that point, the truth of the Trinity comes alive for us. We start with the fact that the early Christians were simply singing a hymn of praise to God for the three basic, dramatic, incredible ways in which they had experienced God: as *Father-Creator, Son-Savior,* and as *Holy Spirit-Sustainer.*

Now, if you were to ask me how I have personally experienced God in my lifetime, I could not express it any better than that. Three amazing ways I have experienced God: God made me; God saved me; God sustains me.

Father, Son, Holy Spirit: one amazing God whom I have experienced in three distinct ways as Creator, Savior, Sustainer. He makes us; He saves us; He sustains us. That's something to sing about. Now let's take a look at these three incredible doxologies.

FIRST, WE SING PRAISE TO THE FATHER-CREATOR

When the early Christians talked about God the Father, they were singing a majestic hymn of praise to the God who created us, and who continues to provide for us. They

41

were saying that God is the Maker of all things, the Lord of all life. But more, they were saying also that he loves his creation like a parent tenderly cares for his or her children.

One day in my searching, I ran across an idea that really spoke to me. It was first suggested by an English philosopher named William Paley, who lived more than 200 years ago. Paley asked you to suppose you are walking across a field one day when suddenly you see a watch on the ground. Imagine that you have never seen a watch before. You pick it up. You examine it. You see the hands moving in an orderly way. You open the watch and discover inside a host of wheels, cogs, springs, jewels, and levers, all ticking away. You notice that things are working together systematically and with purpose. Now what would you think? How would you size this up? Would you say, "Isn't this amazing how all these things (the metal, the glass, the springs, the levers, the wheels) all fell together by chance, and by chance wound themselves up, and by chance made themselves into a watch that keeps perfect time!" No! That's not what you would say at all. Rather, you would say, "I have found a watch. Somewhere there must be a watchmaker!" So, when we find a universe that has an order more accurate, more purposeful, more dependable, and more systematic than we could even imagine, it is natural to say, "We have found a world. Somewhere there must be a world-maker!" Order implies mind. There must be a mind behind it all.

But, there is more. God is not just a world-maker who winds her up and lets her go. No! He not only made us. He made us out of love and for love. The noted poet James Weldon Johnson expressed it beautifully in his epic poem "The Creation." I can just imagine James Earl Jones reciting this with his magnificent and distinctive voice, describing how God made the world out of love and how he took a lump of clay and worked with it and molded it into a person and shaped it in his own image. And then the poem ends with these powerful words,

Then into it He blew the breath of life,
And man became a living soul.

The God who made the universe created you and me. The God who created the world loves you and me. If you ever wonder about that, look at your fingerprints. Your fingerprints are unique; different from anybody else's who ever lived or ever will live. God put his distinct stamp of love on you, and made you special, because you are special to him.

If you still wonder about that, look at Jesus. And that brings us to point two.

SECOND, WE SING PRAISE TO THE SON-SAVIOR

Remember the story about the little girl who was drawing a picture? Her mother walked by and asked her what she was drawing. Without looking up, the little girl answered confidently, "I'm drawing a picture of God." "But, Honey," the mother said, "how can you do that? Nobody knows what God looks like." The little girl said, "Well, they will when I get through."

Jesus paints the portrait of God. He shows us what God is like and what God wants us to be like. And the word describing what we should be like is *love!* God's incredible love not only makes us; it also saves us.

Remember the story about the man who had been known around town as a reprobate and a drunkard? But then Christ came into his life and saved him. Christ changed him completely and turned his life around. His coworkers noticed the change in him and they tried to tease him, shake him, and challenge his faith. "Surely, you don't buy all that stuff in the Bible about miracles, do you?" they said to him. "Surely, you don't really believe Jesus turned water into wine." "Whether he turned water into wine or not," said the man, "I don't know. I wasn't there. But I do know this: in my own house, I have seen him turn beer into furniture, whiskey into food, and tears into laughter!"

Now, I want to say something to you with all the feeling I have in my heart: I hope you become a great success. You can make a lot of money, you can rise to places of prominence in the world, you can have all the symbols of affluence, but if you don't have Christ in your heart as your personal Savior, your life will be an empty shell. Only those who learn how to live and love in the spirit of Christ are truly successful!

As Christians, we sing praise to the Father-Creator, to the Son-Savior.

THIRD, WE SING PRAISE TO THE HOLY SPIRIT-SUSTAINER

God makes us. God saves us. He also sustains us. He does not desert us. He does not leave us alone. He gives us his Holy Spirit to guide us, inspire us, strengthen us, comfort us, and encourage us.

Recently, I spent some time with an amazing family. They have gone through so much trouble, disappointment, and heartache in the last few years, and yet they continue to inspire everyone who knows them with their incredible strength and courage. How do they do it? Well, many people have asked them that question. Their answer is always the same: "God is with us and he will see us through." God is with us. That is the good news of our faith. From cover to cover, that is the message of the Bible. *God is with us.*

Now, let me conclude with an anonymously authored dialogue between God and someone like you and me:

And the Lord said, "Go!"

And I said, "Who, me?"

And he said, "Yes, you."

And I said, "But, Lord, I'm not ready yet. I'm not prepared yet. I'm not psyched up yet. Besides I'm needed here."

And God said, "You're stalling." Again, the Lord said, "Go!"

And I said, "But I don't want to."

46

And he said, "I didn't ask if you wanted to."

And I said, "Listen, Lord. I'm not that kind of person. I'm not talented enough to represent you. I'm not good enough. I don't want to get into controversy. Besides, my family may not like this. And what will the neighbors say?"

And God said, "You're stalling again."

And yet a third time, the Lord said, "Go!"

And I said "Do I have to?"

And he said, "Do you love me?"

And I said, "Lord, you know I love you. But look — I'm scared. People are going to ridicule me and cut me into little pieces. And I just can't take that all by myself."

And God said, "Where do you think I'll be?" Again the Lord said, "Go! And I will go with you!"

And I prayed, "Here am I, Lord. Send me."

That's what it's all about. Every doctrine was first a doxology; every belief was first a song — a song of praise to God. So don't get lost in the questions and complexities. Just join in the song. Praise be to the God who makes us, who saves us, who sustains us. Praise be to the Father, the Son, and the Holy Spirit.

CHAPTER FOUR:
THE PRIORITY OF THE
PRINCE OF PEACE

SCRIPTURE: MARK 5:1–20;
JOHN 16:25–33

It is always sad when nations go to war. In recent years the sadness has been magnified because as recently as the 1990s, we seemed so close to a lasting peace.

The wall had gone down in Berlin. Eastern Europe had opened up. The cold war with Russia had thawed. And at that time in the early 1990s, we thought, "Finally! At long last, we can have a peaceful world." But then suddenly on August 2, 1990, Iraq invaded Kuwait launching a crescendo of tension-packed events that led to the first Gulf War. Then, eleven years later, we experienced the horror and tragedy and heartrending pain of September 11, 2001, which led to the War on Terror, prompting military action in Afghanistan and Iraq. And during those dramatic days, unforgettable images captured our minds and touched our hearts.

For example:

- The image of people by the thousands coming to kneel at the altar of our churches to pray for peace, joining hundreds of thousands of people around the globe in peace prayer vigils.
- The image of a grandmother leaving our sanctuary one Sunday and asking us to pray especially for her grandson who is a jet pilot stationed somewhere in Iraq, constantly in harm's way.
- The image of a little preschool girl saying on television, "I wish we didn't have wars because people get hurt."
- The image of world leaders and congressional leaders and people in the streets agreeing that something should be done, but strongly disagreeing over how to do it.
- The image of the president speaking to the nation and the world from the Oval Office.
- The image of one young soldier shown wearing four different crosses sent to him by different friends and relatives and then saying, "In foxholes, there are no atheists." And the image of another young marine wearing around his neck a piece of debris from the World Trade Center.
- The image of courageous TV and radio

news correspondents giving the news in dangerous situations and then scurrying to safety or frantically helping each other put on gas masks.

- The image of two little girls crying because their mother is in the military and is stationed in harm's way in the Middle East.
- The image of seeing war, as never before, on live television.

On and on we could go with a moving and poignant litany of these powerful images etched indelibly into our hearts and minds. Now, I don't want to be overly dramatic or sensationalistic but I do think we need to grapple with this together. I do think we need to try to bring some spiritual light to the situation.

Let me admit up front that I am certainly no authority on this complex matter and I do not pretend to be. Back during the 1960s a reporter asked Elvis Presley what was his solution regarding the war in Vietnam. Elvis answered, "Ma'am, I just sing songs." In like manner, I just preach sermons, and I know less about war than Elvis did. But something needs to be said today, so let me give it a try.

Over the years as I have studied the Bible,

Christian theology and history, I have noticed that broadly speaking, there are four basic approaches to war. Let me briefly and simply outline them and you see if you can find yourself and your view somewhere between the lines.

First, there is the "Holy War approach." Holy war advocates believe strongly that their war is of God, that their military crusade is divinely ordained and divinely inspired. The holy war crusaders are absolutely certain that their convictions are right because they believe firmly that they are fighting for God. Many wars in history have started with this kind of religious fervor.

One of the most tragic examples of the Holy War mind-set occurred in the Middle Ages when a group of 20,000 children (some of them no more than twelve years of age) became convinced that God wanted them to wage a military crusade. They marched off to war never to return. Many were killed and the others were sold into slavery.

And then, there is always that haunting question, What if both sides believe they are doing God's will? Once, when war broke out, one of our military leaders was asked, "Is war of God, or is it of Satan?" Soberly he answered, "It's of man!"

A second approach to war is called "pacifism." Of course, the basic premise of the pacifist position is that there is no such thing as holy war. "All war is unholy and immoral," says the pacifist. The view here is that violence of any kind is utterly unchristian. The pacifist maintains that if you really search the mind of Christ and think deeply about the meaning of Christian love, the conclusion you come to is that violence, force, and killing are incompatible with discipleship.

However, the arguments that the pacifists have to wrestle with are obvious:

- What do you do when someone invades your home and threatens to do harm to you and your family?
- What do you do when someone abuses an innocent and defenseless country?
- How do you deal with the aggressor?
- How do you resist what is evil or hostile or wrong?

This brings us to a third approach which some have labeled the "Just War." The basic premise here is that war is always a tragedy, and should always be a last resort. Every effort at negotiation should be tried. Yet, when these fail, there are occasions, say the just war advocates, when war becomes necessary.

Thomas Aquinas, in the thirteenth century, said that a just war must satisfy three conditions: it must be declared by public authorities, the cause must indeed be just, and the motive must be right.

During World War II, Bishop William Temple expressed the Just War philosophy when he said this: "We Christians in wartime are called to the hardest of all tasks: to fight without hatred, to resist without bitterness, and in the end . . . to triumph without vindictiveness."

A new element, which has been currently brought into the Just War approach, is called "Humane Fighting." Humane Fighting sounds like a contradiction, doesn't it? But what it means is that force should be directed only toward the destruction of armaments. Innocent lives should be protected as much as possible. "Take out their weapons!" Instead of wholesale attacks on a nation without regard for the civilian population, use surgical, precision strikes to destroy their military weapons. Render them weaponless, and then they will come to talk peace.

Of course, the problem here is that it's impossible to employ that much force and only take out hardware. Casualties will occur on both sides. And when the casualty happens, it will be somebody's son or daughter, somebody's wife or husband, somebody's dad or mom.

Now, a fourth approach to war has emerged in recent years because of the advent of modern weapons and the frightening threat of nuclear power. It's called "Waging War by Sanctions." We have heard a lot about this in recent years. The idea here is that military force is too dangerous and too destructive, and a better way to deal with the problem is to cut the troublesome nation off from international supplies. Cut them off from the world and weaken them in that way, to the point that they have to come to the peace table. Well, we've all heard the pros and cons of this sanctions approach in Congress in recent years.

Now, what do you think? Where do you stand? Are you a crusader, a pacifist, a Just War advocate, or someone who believes we can wage war with international sanctions?

By the way, this very day, I have Christian friends who strongly subscribe to each one of these different positions, and they all base their view on their Christian faith and they all document their approach with Scripture. So, it can be very confusing. And yet in the complexity and perplexity of it all, I do see some important lessons begging to be learned. I hope and pray that all of our soldiers, wherever they may be, can come safely home very soon, but as we go through war and on beyond it, I hope we will think about these things.

FIRST, MORE THAN EVER WE SHOULD REALIZE THAT OUR WORLD HAS BECOME A GLOBAL VILLAGE

Because of the amazing advances in travel and telecommunications, we have become a global village. We live in a rapidly shrinking world. With every passing day, especially because of television satellites, we become more and more aware of one another and our lives become more and more inter-related with people around the world.

The lesson is obvious. We in the world must stop seeing other nations as enemies and, rather, see them as neighbors with whom we share our global village. If you have any doubts about that, let me document it.

Some years ago, I was watching an ABC newscast. A news correspondent was interviewing one of the highest-ranking officials in Saudi Arabia. The conversation was sober, serious, businesslike, until the Saudi official suddenly heard a familiar sound on his earphone. Suddenly, the Saudi official became very animated, very excited, and then this conversation took place:

"Wait a minute! Wait a minute!" said the Saudi official. "Was that Ted Koppel's voice I just heard?"

"Yes."

"May I say hello to Ted?"

"Of course."

"Ted Koppel, is that really you? I watch you every night. You are great! Keep up the good work. I can't wait to get home tonight to tell my family I talked to Ted Koppel!"

That Saudi official was like a kid in a candy store, so thrilled to hear the voice of Ted Koppel, a television celebrity he watched every night.

Also, have you noticed that when some new development occurs in the war, leaders of nations all over the world are watching CNN to see what really happened? CNN is giving news to the world even faster than national intelligence agencies can get the scoop.

A couple of years ago when our travel group toured China, we visited a Chinese kindergarten. They performed Chinese songs for us in their native language. Then their teacher, who could speak a little English, asked us to perform for them. Since the kindergarten was connected to a farm, we sang, "Old McDonald Had a Farm." When we finished that first line, guess what those Chinese kindergartners did. They shouted back to us, "E-I-E-I-O."

We live in a global village. No question about it. And we need to see other nations and other peoples as neighbors and not enemies. Even though we may not understand other nations' leaders and the things they do, we must not permit ourselves to hate these nations' people, because they, too, are God's children, and they, too, are our neighbors in God's global village called Earth.

SECOND, PEOPLE IN OUR WORLD MAY SEEM SO VERY DIFFERENT, BUT FUNDAMENTALLY WE ARE SO SIMILAR

Our languages may be different; our clothes may be different; our customs may be different; our physical traits may be different;

our worship may be different; but the truth is, basically, we are pretty much the same. The common people, the people on the street, the regular folks like you and me in every nation are very similar.

I have not traveled as extensively as some people, but I have been to England, Belgium, Germany, Russia, France, Israel, Jordan, Greece, Japan, Egypt, China, Italy, Turkey, Canada, Mexico, Spain, Portugal, Singapore, the Scandinavian countries, not to mention even Waxahachie, Texas; and everywhere I have been, I have discovered that the people in every nation are so much alike. They love their children. They are concerned about health care, education, and food for their tables. They worship, they pray, and they do not want war.

Recently, in our sanctuary, we hosted a worship service for unity. People were here from many different cultures, nationalities, and backgrounds. Greeks, Italians, African Americans, Hispanics; even some native Texans were here. It was a touching, moving experience and I found myself thinking not about how different we are, but rather how alike we are. God must have loved variety; he made so much of it. And yet deep within us, there is an incredible kindred spirit, an amazing alikeness that comes from being brothers and sisters in God's family.

There has been a lot of talk in recent years about how economics relates to war. "Is this conflict over aggression or is it over oil?" some have asked. The debate rages. Let me invite you to think about the economics of it all in another way. Dream with me for a moment. If we in this world could somehow learn how to get along, just think what we could do. If we didn't have to spend so much time, effort, energy, creativity, and money on defending ourselves from one another, just think what we could do. If all the nations of this world could learn to live together in peace without the threat of war, we could take those incredible resources and wage war on hunger, homelessness, disease, illiteracy, and drug abuse. I know it sounds idealistic. I know it sounds like the impossible dream, but I can't help thinking about it. Just think what could be done.

THIRD, THE MOST IMPORTANT LESSON OF ALL: JESUS CHRIST IS THE PRINCE OF PEACE

I believe with all my heart that the way to a lasting peace resides in Jesus Christ — in what he came for and stood for and died for; in his intense pursuit of truth, love, and justice. That is precisely what this story in

Mark 5 is all about. Christ walks into the tormented life of the Gerasene demoniac, this madman, who is at war with everybody and whose life is coming apart at the seams, and Jesus turns it around for him. He gives him the healing he needs, and brings peace to his troubled soul.

At the beginning of this narrative, it sounds like a horror story. This wild-eyed, adrenaline-filled madman comes running and shrieking out of the tombs. This is an eerie, grim, suspenseful situation. Jesus and his disciples have just come through a storm on the Sea of Galilee. It is nighttime and having survived that frightening storm, they are thrilled to now set foot on solid ground. But as they get out of the boat, they encounter a different kind of storm, yet another scary experience. They hear strange sounds coming from the tombs: shrieks, growls, screams, moans, the rattling of chains. Then suddenly, a horrifying sight! A madman in tattered clothes, bruised, dirty, bloody, and battered, with pieces of chains dangling from his arms and ankles, comes running and screaming directly toward them.

Now, let me ask you something: what would you have done in that situation? This was a perilous place, a bloodcurdling moment, with a powerful, dangerous, berserk man charging Jesus and his disciples. I think I would have run for my life or jumped back in the boat. But not Jesus! Jesus stood his ground and faced the madman, undaunted and unafraid. Jesus stood there and dealt with this wild man. Jesus healed him. Jesus brought peace to his troubled soul. He changed him; cleansed him. Jesus turned his life around. And you know, don't you, that he can do that for you and me, and he can do that for our world.

Please notice something here. The madman said his name was Legion. That's a military word, and so appropriate in this case because this man was at war. He was at war with himself. He was at war with other people. He was at war with God. And Jesus, the Prince of Peace, healed him. Jesus, the Prince of Peace, gave him peace within, peace with others, and peace with God.

He can do that for you and me. And he can do that for our world, which today is so like Legion, so desperately in need of peace within, peace with others, and peace with God. Remember how he put it in John 16: "In the world you have tribulation. Be courageous, for I have overcome the world" (v. 33, author's translation). This means that Christ endured the worst this world can dish out and was victorious over it. This means that what he represented cannot be defeated. His truth cannot be killed; it resurrects! His love cannot be stopped; it endures! God cannot be defeated; ultimately he wins, and through faith in him, the Peace, the Healing, the Victory, the New Life can be ours. And this is why it is so crucial, so vital, with the help of God to make Jesus Christ the Prince of Peace the priority of your life.

CHAPTER FIVE:
THE PRIORITY OF
CHRISTLIKENESS

SCRIPTURE: MARK 15:33–41

Each year on Good Friday at St. Luke's United Methodist Church in Houston, Texas, the chancel choir gives a magnificent performance of Théodore Dubois' sacred cantata "The Seven Last Words of Christ," a moving musical presentation of the seven sayings of Christ while he was being crucified on Good Friday. How many of those seven last words can you remember?

- First, he prays for his executioners: "Father, forgive them; they know not what they do."
- Second, he says to the thief on the cross, "Today you will be with me in paradise."
- Third, he provides for the care of his mother through the disciple John as he says, "Woman, behold your son," and to John he says, "Behold your mother"; meaning, "Mother, from this point

64

forward John will be like a son to you. John will take care of you."

- Fourth, there is the lament from Psalm 22, "My God, why hast Thou forsaken me?"
- Fifth, there is the cry "I thirst!"
- Sixth, there is the prayerful "Father, into Thy hands I commend my spirit."
- Seventh, there is the triumphant shout, "It is finished."

Now, of those seven words from the cross, at least three of them are prayers; three of them are addressed to God: "Father, forgive them; they know not what they do." "My God, why hast Thou forsaken me?" and "Father, into Thy hands I commit my spirit."

Let's take a quick look at each one of these Cross Prayers, because in them we find the crux of the Christian gospel.

FIRST, "FATHER, FORGIVE THEM; THEY KNOW NOT WHAT THEY DO"

As Jesus utters this prayer, time stands still, because this is one of the greatest moments in all of human history, one of the highest mountain peaks in all of the Bible. It is the picture of unconditional love. It is the portrait of amazing grace. It is the measur-

65

ing stick by which we gauge our forgiveness of others.

If you ever wonder, "Should I forgive that person who has wronged me or hurt me?" If that question "Should I forgive?" ever comes into your mind, just remember the image of Jesus hanging there, nailed to a cross totally innocent, and saying, "Father, forgive them."

Sam was a sixteen-year-old high school freshman. He was a remarkable person — kind and compassionate and committed to Christ. His Christian faith was radiant and winsome. He could light up a room with his warm smile. Everybody loved Sam. But then tragedy struck. It was the end of the spring semester. The high school yearbook had come out. Sam was a freshman, and he was so proud and excited to receive his first yearbook. Sam was in the cafeteria signing people's yearbooks and having them sign his. It was a happy moment. However, when Sam came out of the cafeteria, one of his classmates, a guy named Jack, tried to snatch the yearbook out of Sam's hands.

Jack couldn't afford to buy a yearbook, so he tried to take Sam's. Sam was a very non-combative person, but it was his first yearbook and he wouldn't let go. Jack lost control, doubled up his fist, and swung as hard as he could. When Sam saw the punch coming and tried to dodge, Jack's fist slammed right into Sam's esophagus, collapsing it, and Sam went down unconscious. They rushed Sam to the hospital for emergency surgery, but it was too late. Sam died on the operating table. It just didn't seem possible. Sixteen years old, and so quickly gone, because of a high school yearbook that cost eight dollars.

That night, friends and relatives gathered in shock and grief at Sam's home. There was a knock at the front door. A person was standing there with a note that read: "Dear Mr. and Mrs. [. . .], I'm so sorry my son killed your son. I'm blind. My husband deserted me. And I'm trying to raise eight children alone. I didn't have eight dollars for a yearbook. Please forgive. (Signed) Jack's mother."

Jack was arrested. When he went to court, his mother could not afford a lawyer to defend her child. And do you know what happened? Sam's parents hired an attorney to represent Jack. When Jack was convicted of second-degree manslaughter and sent to the youth detention center, it was Sam's parents who visited him; it was Sam's parents who took Jack's mother to visit her child. It was Sam's parents who called him on the phone and wrote him letters of encouragement. And when Jack was finally released, Sam's parents were there to pick him up and take him home to his mother.

That's an amazing story about the incredible spirit of forgiveness. Let me ask you something. Can you forgive like that? Do you have that spirit of forgiveness in you? You know where Sam's parents got that spirit, don't you? They got it from Jesus Christ. They got it from Holy Week. They got it from Good Friday. They got it from the One who was nailed to a cross and said, "Father, forgive them." It's hard to forgive like that, but it's also great because it is so Christlike. That's the first prayer of Christ on the cross: "Father, forgive them; they know not what they do."

SECOND, "MY GOD, WHY HAST THOU FORSAKEN ME?"

At first glance, many folks read this and wish it weren't in the Bible because it sounds so unlike Jesus. Yet here it is. So what are we to make of it? A closer look reveals that there is something very precious here. Let's see if we can find it.

Over the years, there have been three classic interpretations that scholars have attached to this poignant verse. The first interpretation is that Jesus is quoting the Twenty-second Psalm to affirm that he is the Messiah foretold by the Old Testament. You see, the Twenty-second Psalm (which was well known to the people of that time) begins with these exact words: "My God, my God, why hast thou forsaken me?" (KJV). And then, interestingly, even though the psalm was written hundreds of years before Good Friday, it describes amazingly the precise events of that infamous day. Following are some words from the Twenty-second Psalm:

> I am . . .
>> scorned by others, and despised by the people.
> All who see me mock at me;
>> they make mouths at me, they shake their heads.
> . . . .
> I am poured out like water,
>> and all my bones are out of joint.
> . . . .
>> a company of evildoers encircles me.
> My hands and feet have shriveled.
> . . . .
> they divide my clothes among themselves,
>> and for my clothing they cast lots. (vv. 6–7, 14, 16–18)

Isn't that amazing? What an accurate description of the crucifixion that was written hundreds of years before it. And then the Twenty-second Psalm bursts into praise: "All the ends of the earth shall remember and turn to the LORD. . . . Future generations will be told about the Lord, and proclaim his deliverance to a people yet unborn" (vv. 27, 30–31).

So it may well be that Jesus was recalling the Twenty-second Psalm on the cross as a picture of what he, himself, was going through, and as a living out of the Old Testament prophecy, and as a song of trust and confidence, knowing full well that though the Twenty-second Psalm began in lament, it ended in triumph and praise.

A second interpretation is that Jesus in his anguish is finding strength by quoting the Twenty-second Psalm. One scholar said that though this is an attractive interpretation, he didn't believe that a person in such agony would be quoting Scripture. The scholar who said that must not be a pastor, and he must not have gone through much agony, because I have found that when we are in pain that's when we quote Scripture the most. Time after time, I have walked into hospital rooms and found people quoting the Twenty-third Psalm or the Lord's Prayer or the Beatitudes.

It is also interesting to note that in every prayer we have that Jesus prayed, he always calls God "Father" except here, which probably means he was quoting another man's prayer, namely, the Twenty-second Psalm.

A third interpretation of this haunting verse is that this prayer came at the precise moment when all the sins of the world were laid on Jesus, at the precise moment when he became the sacrificial lamb to save us from our sins, at the precise moment when he who knew no sin bore our sins. You know, we could make a good case for this interpretation, because biblically, sin does mean "separation from God." And the Bible does say by his stripes we are healed.

One day a man decided to take a shortcut across a muddy field, but he slipped and fell into a deep pit. He tried his best to get out with his own strength, but he couldn't make it. So he began to cry out for someone to save him.

A pop psychologist passed by and said, "I feel your pain. I empathize with your life down there in the pit."

A TV talk show host came by and said, "When you get out — if you get out — you can come and be on my show."

A religious fanatic happened along and

said, "You must have sinned a great sin because only bad people fall into pits."

A news reporter rushed up to him and said, "Could I have an exclusive story on your experience in the pit?"

A lawyer came out from town and wanted to represent the man in a lawsuit.

An IRS agent came to see if he had paid his taxes on the pit.

A neurotic came along and said, "You think *your* pit is bad; you should see *mine.*"

An optimist said, "Things could be worse."

A pessimist said, "Things will get worse!"

Then another person came along. He saw the man's dilemma, and his heart went out to him. He reached down with both hands and, with strength and grace, pulled the man up and out of the pit. The rescued man thanked the kind stranger and then ran into town to tell everyone what had happened, how he had been saved. "How did you get out?" they asked.

"A man reached down and pulled me out," he said.

"Who was the man?" they asked.

"It was Jesus," he replied.

"How do you know that?" they questioned.

"I knew it," he said, "because he had nail

prints in his hands." (Adapted from Kenneth D. Filkins in *Frogs in Cream* by Stephen Gaukroger and Nick Mercer.)

You see, we don't have to reinvent the wheel when it comes to salvation. We don't have to chase every new fad that comes along. All we have to do is take hold of those nail-scarred hands.

THIRD, "FATHER, INTO THY HANDS I COMMEND MY SPIRIT"

Did you know that this was not the first time Jesus had prayed this prayer, "Father, into Thy hands I commend my spirit." He had likely prayed it hundreds of times as a child, because this was the bedtime prayer taught to little children during biblical times. It was the first-century version of "Now I lay me down to sleep, I pray the Lord my soul to keep." "Father, I'm about to go to sleep, so into thy hands I commit my spirit. I'm going to sleep now, Father. I know you are here to watch over me."

It was the prayer of total and complete trust. It was the prayer of total and complete confidence. It was the prayer Jesus prayed on the cross just before he breathed his last. And it is the prayer you and I can pray daily because we know that we can trust God, because we know that God has the power to turn the agony of Good Friday into the ecstasy of Easter Sunday; that God has the power to resurrect; that God has the power to take the cross (the emblem of suffering and shame) and turn it into the greatest symbol of victory this world has ever known. We can pray that prayer because we know not what the future holds, but we know who holds the future.

Chapter Six:
The Priority of the
Holy Spirit

SCRIPTURE: ACTS 2:37–42

A little girl was visiting her grandmother one beautiful spring morning. They walked out into Grandmother's flower garden. As Grandmother was inspecting the progress of her flowers, the little girl decided to try to open a rosebud with her own two hands. But no luck. As she would pull the petals open, they would tear or bruise or wilt or break off completely. Finally, in frustration, she said, "Gramma, I just don't understand it at all. When God opens a flower, it looks so beautiful, but when I try, it just comes apart."

"Well, honey," Grandmother answered, "There's a good reason for that. God is able to do it because he works from the inside out!"

"God works from the inside out." That is the great message of Pentecost Sunday, isn't it? This is what the disciples finally came to understand at Pentecost. Jesus had ascended into heaven. And he had told the disciples to wait in Jerusalem for the Holy Spirit.

Here is where the story of Pentecost picks up. The disciples are back in the Upper Room waiting and wondering. And some of them were probably grumbling impatiently and nervously, "What in the world are we doing here? All this waiting around is driving me up the wall! There's no use. He's gone and without him, we are nothing. It's over! We'd just as well face it. What is this Holy Spirit business anyway? Maybe we misunderstood him."

Just then they heard a sound. The breath of God began to blow on that place like the rush of a mighty wind. Images of fire danced around them. Suddenly, their fear was gone, replaced by peace and confidence, courage and strength and unity. And they began to speak and communicate the word of God boldly. Amazingly, people from all different backgrounds heard and responded, and 3,000 people were converted that day.

It's interesting to note that the three classic symbols for the Holy Spirit in the Bible remind us of how God works through us and how God works from the inside out.

Do you remember what they are? The three traditional symbols of the Holy Spirit in the Bible are:

- breath, the symbol of life and vitality
- fire, the symbol of power
- the descending dove, the symbol of peace

Let's take a look at these one at a time.

FIRST, THERE IS BREATH, THE SYMBOL OF LIFE AND VITALITY

Remember in the garden of Eden when God created Adam and Eve? He shaped them, but they were lifeless until he breathed into their nostrils the breath of life. They didn't really come alive until he breathed his spirit into them. Again, we see it here at Pentecost. The Breath of God, like the rush of a mighty wind, blew upon that place, and the disciples came alive.

I was watching the National Basketball Association play-offs on television one evening. After the game, the coach of the losing team was being interviewed. He was not happy with the way his team played and he said, "We deserved to get beat because we were absolutely listless out there tonight. We had no drive, no emotion. We were like zombies, just going through the motions. We had no life at all!" And then he said, "We had no spirit!"

As he said that, it made me think that

that's how some people go through life spiritually; absolutely listless with no zest, no commitment, no drive, no fervor. Like robots, they stonewall through the days just going through the motions of living, but not really living at all. They have blocked the Holy Spirit of God out of their lives, and they are not really living at all!

How is it with you? Is God in your life? Is the Holy Spirit in your soul? Has God's spirit breathed on you the breath of real life? If not, you are not really living! You may be existing, coping. You may be floating along, but until the Holy Spirit comes into your heart, you are numbered among the lifeless; you are numbered among the walking dead.

Edwin Hatch years ago recognized the importance of this, and he wrote these words:

Breathe on me, Breath of God,
Fill me with life anew,
That I may love what Thou dost love,
And do what Thou wouldst do.

The first sign of the Holy Spirit in the Bible is breath, the symbol of life and zest and vitality. The kind of life created only by the Presence of God.

SECOND, THERE IS FIRE, THE SYMBOL OF POWER

We often put the words *fire* and *power* together, don't we? We talk about *firepower.* In the Bible, fire is often used as the symbol of God's presence and power. For example, we see it in the burning bush of Exodus and again here in the New Testament story of Pentecost.

Have you heard the story about the man who had been suffering with a headache for several days? Finally, he went to see a doctor. However, the office nurse who looked and acted like a marine drill sergeant at Parris Island greeted him gruffly. When he told her about his headache, she barked in a loud stern voice, "Go into that examination room, take off your clothes, and put on this hospital gown. The doctor will be there in a few minutes."

The man protested, "But Ma'am, I really don't need to go through all of that. I just have this chronic headache."

To which the nurse answered, "Sir, did you hear what I said? You go into that examination room and put on that hospital gown right now!"

And so the man did. When he got into the room and closed the door, he discovered another man already sitting in there wearing a hospital gown. The man with the headache said to the other guy, "This is ridiculous. I don't know what in the world I'm doing in here. This is crazy. I just have a headache."

The other man said, "You think *you've* got problems. I just came in here to read the meter!"

Now, that nurse had power, didn't she? But that's not the kind of power I'm talking about — not the power of brute force or blatant intimidation; not the power of political clout or wealth or weapons. But rather, I'm talking about the power of knowing God's presence in our lives, and what that presence produces: integrity, honesty, commitment to a great cause. The sense of being God's coworker, the assurance of God's love; there is nothing stronger than that. That's the firepower of Pentecost that fuels and mobilizes and energizes us and enables us to do great things. There is incredible power in being totally convinced that God is with us and for us, and that he will ultimately win, and that nothing, not even death, can separate us from him.

In the early days of Christianity, the Christians were under heavy persecution. A young Christian man was brought before the Roman governor because he refused to

renounce his God, and he refused to proclaim Caesar as his Lord. The Roman
governor was impressed with the commitment of the young man, and he felt some
compassion for the young Christian. The
governor told him to just renounce his God
and bow down to Caesar and then the
Romans would immediately release him and
set him free and that no harm would come
to him and he could go on his way. But, the
young Christian was unwavering in his faith,
saying to the Roman governor, "I am sorry,
Sir, but I cannot do that. I cannot deny my
God." Amazed, the governor told him that
he could be in big trouble over this, that he
could even lose his life. "Yes," answered the
young Christian, "but I cannot lose my
God!"

Do you know what that young Christian
was saying? He was saying, "I have the
firepower of Pentecost!" Do you have that
kind of power and strength?

THIRD, THERE IS THE DESCENDING
DOVE, THE SYMBOL OF PEACE

The early Christians in creating this symbol
were very wise to show the dove descending
because peace does indeed come from
above. Inner peace — the poise, the serenity, the courage, the confidence to meet life

and its troubles with steady eyes — comes from the presence of the Holy Spirit in our hearts.

Three times this past week, I was reminded of this. Three different conversations with three different families revealed vividly the peace that comes from having God in your life:

- A young couple facing a nightmare experience beyond description in the sudden illness of their baby
- An older couple dealing with the bad news of a medical report and considering their alternatives
- A heartbroken woman grappling with the abrupt loss of her husband of over fifty years

All of them displayed a peace that passes understanding, a peace that comes only from the presence of God in their lives.

Some years ago a teacher asked the students in her fourth-grade class to name the person they considered the greatest person alive in the world today. Their responses were varied and interesting.

One little boy said, "I think it's Tom Brady because he led the Patriots to all those Super Bowl wins." A little girl said Brad

Pitt, and still another girl named Oprah. On and on it went with the students mentioning a wide variety of celebrities.

But then it was little Donnie's turn. Without hesitation Donnie said, "I think it's Jesus Christ because he loves everybody and is always ready to help them." Mrs. Thompson smiled and said, "Well, I certainly like your answer, Donnie, because I'm a Christian too, and I also admire Jesus very much. But there's one slight problem. I said the greatest *living* person, and of course, Jesus lived and died almost two thousand years ago. Do you have another name in mind?" I love the simple, innocent, confident, wide-eyed response of little Donnie. He said, "Oh, no, Mrs. Thompson, that's not right at all. Jesus Christ is alive! He lives in me right now!"

That's the good news of our faith: God is with us right now working from the inside out, giving us the breath of life, the firepower of commitment, and the peace that passes all understanding.

CHAPTER SEVEN:
THE PRIORITY OF
GRATITUDE TO GOD
SCRIPTURE: LUKE 17:11–19

In the summer of 1620 a sizable group of adventuresome citizens set out on two ships from Southampton, England, with the full intention of establishing a settlement in the Virginia Colony in this new world called America. As they sailed around the southern tip of the British Isles, however, one of the boats called the *Speedwell* had problems that made it unseaworthy, so they were forced to stop. Those who still wanted to make the journey crowded onto a ship called the *Mayflower* and then they set out to sea once again.

The trip took much longer than they had anticipated — sixty-six days — and since their instruments for navigation were very primitive, unbeknownst to them they were blown off course. When they finally sighted land, it was not the Virginia Colony at all, but what we now call Massachusetts.

They had hoped to arrive in time to build

shelters before the winter set in, but by now it was almost December. They sent scouting parties ashore. They were able with great difficulty to construct shelters of a sort, but they were really quite inadequate against the brutal elements of that region.

Overexposure led to diseases of all kinds, and before the spring finally came exactly half of the 102 people who had made the trip had died and were buried in unmarked graves because they did not want the Native Americans to know how decimated their ranks had become. There was not a family in the community that did not lose at least one of its own during that first terrible winter. When spring did come, what was left of the crew of the *Mayflower* prepared to return to England, because the *Mayflower* was a rented ship. This led to a serious discussion about whether the whole project should just be abandoned, and whether the surviving pilgrims should just all get on the ship and go back with the crew.

However, in a gesture of real courage and hope, they decided to stay on. With the help of some friendly Native Americans, they planted about 30 acres of grain. They were able also to build more substantial shelters for themselves and when fall came, the harvest was incredible, more abundant than anything they had ever known in the old country.

As the time for the first anniversary of their landing in this new world approached, a discussion arose as to how they should commemorate this occasion. There were two schools of thought. Some felt strongly that they should make it a day of mourning. After all, the losses during that first year had been staggering, and a day to remember all of those who had died seemed to be in order. However, others felt strongly that it should be a day of thanksgiving. Even though they had lost a great deal, it was also clear that they had so much to be grateful for. After all, they had survived. Their future seemed now to be secure. The Native Americans had been surprisingly kind and helpful. And the land had proved to be fertile beyond their wildest imagination.

Why not focus on thanksgiving rather than mourning? The debate went on and on between these two alternatives: Should it be a day of mourning or a day of thanksgiving? Of course, as we know from subsequent history, the "Thanksgiving party" won out.

This one decision by those early pilgrims may have had as much to do with the future development of our country as any other one thing, because in every situation we always have this choice:

- Will we mourn or will we give thanks?
- Will we groan and gripe and complain or will we express gratitude?
- Will we focus on the problems or the opportunities?
- Will we underscore all the things that are going against us or will we celebrate all the things that are going for us?
- Will we be "trouble-collectors" or "thanks-givers"?

In Luke 17:11–19, Jesus shows us that it is so crucial to choose the way of gratitude, that it is so important to stop and say thanks. Remember the story with me.

Jesus was on his way to Jerusalem. As he entered a village, he was met by ten lepers. They had heard about him and his power to heal, so they cried out to him for help. He told them to go and show themselves to the priests, and as they went they were all cleansed! All ten were healed, but only one of them stopped to say thanks. Jesus commended him and then asked, "Where are the other nine?" The point of the story is clear: it's a beautiful thing to stop and express thanksgiving, but many people never really realize that, because they are giving so much time and energy to complaining about their problems.

Can't you just hear the other nine?

"Sure, I'm glad to be healed but why did I have to have the leprosy in the first place?"

"Maybe he didn't have anything to do with it. Maybe the healing just came on its own."

"Perhaps I should go back but I may not be able to find him. And besides that, I'm not wasting any more time on this illness; it's already taken enough time out of my life."

This choice between being a trouble-collector or a thanks-giver is so crucial. It determines in large part who we are and how we live, and the state of our spiritual health. When Jesus said to the leper who came back, "Your faith has made you well," at least a part of what he meant was, "Your gratitude has made you well," because being able to celebrate life and say thanks to God is a tremendous indicator of our spiritual wholeness. I like the way this reads in the King James Version. Jesus says to the grateful man with leprosy, "Thy faith hath made thee whole." Ten were made well, but only this one became whole.

I remember very well when I got my first inkling of this important truth. I was six or seven years old. It was the Sunday before Thanksgiving. My Sunday school teacher held up a glass of water and said, "Boys and girls, I have a question for you. Is this a glass of water half-empty or half-full?" One student said, "Half-empty." Another said, "No, it is half-full." The teacher said, "Technically, you are both right. It is half-empty; it is also half-full. But the way you look at it makes all the difference in the world. If you focus on the half-emptiness, you will feel discouraged and negative because you will always wish that there were more. But, on the other hand, if you focus on the half-fullness, it will give you a sense of delight and gladness and gratefulness. Boys and girls, I hope all of your life, every single day, you will focus on the half-fullness — and not the half-emptiness."

I have never forgotten that simple but profound Sunday school object lesson. The choice is ours every day in every situation. We can groan over what we don't have — or we can give thanks for what we do have. Let me break this down a bit and show you what I mean.

FIRST, THE CHOICE IS OURS: WE CAN ENCOURAGE OR DISCOURAGE

Back in the mid-1940s, a little church in Alabama had every reason to be discouraged. They very rarely had 100 people in attendance. They didn't have a lot of money in that community, and the town was not growing, but this little church family kept on hanging in there and doing the best they could.

Many people would have said, "What's the use? We can't do much. We might as well have a day of mourning and shut the church down. It's just so discouraging trying to keep this church going and pay the bills when there are so few of us and our resources are so meager. What difference does it make anyway?" But that little church in Alabama refused to give up. They would not give in to discouragement. They kept on coming. They paid the utility bills. They took care of their pastor. They kept the church alive and going. They bought the Sunday school literature, and they helped a small group of children and teenagers learn something about Jesus.

On December 19, 1943, at 7:30 p.m. they had a Christmas pageant. Let me tell you about the children in that Christmas play: one little girl grew up to become a foreign missionary. Another grew up to become a pastor's wife. Two others grew up to be a campus pastor and a pastor in Florida. Also in that Christmas pageant cast were two little boys who would become the pastors of one of the finest United Methodist churches and one of the finest Baptist churches in America.

One of those little boys (now older), reflecting on that, said, "The Lord only knows where I'd be standing today — probably not in a pulpit — if not for the encouragement I received from that little church in Alabama long ago." That little church had lots to be discouraged about, but they would not give in to that. They saw the glass half-full, not half-empty. And they chose the way of encouragement, and God took it from there and did great things. That choice is ours, too, isn't it? We can encourage or we can discourage.

SECOND, THE CHOICE IS OURS: WE CAN LAUGH OR LAMENT

Some people go miserably through life, crying, "Woe is me," at every turn. But you see, that is so sad because God meant life to be joyous. A good sense of humor is so important. We need to learn how to laugh, especially at ourselves, and not take ourselves so seriously.

I probably shouldn't tell you this, but I will: I find it interesting to watch the bridal party at weddings. It is a nervous, emotional time, and those who know how to laugh fare much better.

Some years ago, I presided at a wedding that turned into a disaster because the bride had no sense of humor. She was determined to have the perfect wedding. She included everything she had ever heard of in her life in the wedding — the works! And she tried so hard to have the super pluperfect wedding that she just upset everybody. Things went along pretty well until time for the nuptial kiss.

As a surprise to the groom (and to me and everybody else), the bride had asked her brother to slip into the choir loft during the closing prayer and just as I said the final "amen" to play (of all things) a tape of the theme from *2001: A Space Odyssey* on his boom box. It came on with such a blast that the maid of honor screamed and jumped back and knocked over a candle. As the best man tried to catch the falling candle, he stepped on the bride's dress. She dropped her flowers and her veil fell off. She stumbled as she turned to go out of the church, the flower girl started to scream and cry, and they forgot the nuptial kiss altogether. By the time the bride and groom reached the back of the church, she was furious and she had decided that it was all the groom's fault, and he couldn't figure out what he had done wrong.

It was the only time in my life that I had to take the bride and groom into a private room to calm them down before they could even go into the reception. I said, "Look, you are married now. That's all that matters. You love each other and want to share all of life together, and you are just as married as any couple that's ever taken those sacred vows. That's what it's all about. All the candles and pageantry — that's just frosting on the cake. There are no perfect weddings and the things that went wrong are just things to laugh about in the years to come. You love each other, and you are married now. That's the important thing."

Put that over against this: a couple got married and the pastor asked the groom, "Will you have this woman to be your wedded wife, to live together in the holy estate of matrimony? Will you love her, comfort her, honor and keep her, in sickness and health, and forsaking all other, keep you only unto her so long as you both shall live?"

The groom was so nervous he said, "Will you repeat the question?" It took a sense of humor to get through that. They have it on audiotape, and every now and then to this day, they take it out and listen to it and laugh. The choice is ours: we can encourage or discourage; we can laugh or lament.

THIRD, THE CHOICE IS OURS: WE CAN CELEBRATE OR COMPLAIN

John Claypool tells a wonderful story out of his own life that makes the point graphically. He tells about going to make pastoral calls at a large hospital. He visited two women both approaching ninety years of age and both with physical difficulties. When John entered the first woman's room, he felt this incredible cloud of despair. The woman was quick to list all of her complaints. The doctors didn't come around often enough. The nurses were inattentive and unsympathetic. She said it was impossible to sleep with all that hospital noise. The sheets were like sandpaper, she said, and the food was terrible.

Claypool said he tried his best to cheer her up, but to no avail. The atmosphere in that room was dark and heavy with depression. Claypool left that room drained and blue.

Two floors down, he saw the other woman who was facing some serious physical ailments, but the atmosphere was totally different. The woman bragged on her doctors. And the nurses were so sweet and competent and helpful. "I love all the attention," she said. "Everybody is so good to me and every time the door opens I can't wait to see what fresh young thing is coming in to check on me."

"Can you sleep?" Claypool asked.

"Oh my, yes. This bed is wonderful and goodness gracious, they change the sheets every day. Isn't that something? I feel like I'm in the lap of luxury here."

"How about the food?" Claypool asked.

"Why, it's delicious," she answered. "They bring it in to me on a tray and I love the variety of the menu." And then she added, "Now, John, eating for me under any circumstances is not easy because at my age I only have two teeth left, but thank the good Lord, they hit!" (John Claypool, Shamblin Lectures, St. Luke's United Methodist Church, Houston, Texas, November 22, 1998).

Claypool said that at that moment he felt like stepping back and giving her a full military salute! All the heroism in the world is not confined to the battlefield. Here was a person who was really up against it, who had every reason to mourn, who had every reason to be discouraged, every reason to lament and to complain. But she had chosen instead to be grateful. She chose to make gratitude a priority in her life.

CHAPTER EIGHT: THE PRIORITY OF SERVICE TO GOD

SCRIPTURE: MARK 1:16–20

I was eight years old when I went to work. It was my first "paying job." My brother Bob was ten and I was eight when we became the delivery boys for Moore's Grocery in Memphis, Tennessee.

Our family owned the grocery store and we all worked in the store. Our dad was the butcher, Mom was the cashier, and Bob and I were the delivery boys. People would call our store and place their orders over the phone, and then Bob and I would deliver their groceries to their homes. We had specially made bicycles with large wire baskets on the front and on the back. We would fill the orders, place the groceries in the baskets on our bikes, and then carry the groceries right into people's kitchens.

Back in those simple days, if someone called in a $20 order, we would have to make two bike trips because, back then, $20 would buy lots of groceries. In between orders, Mom and Dad would let Bob and me play outside. We loved sports, so we would always get up a game of whatever sport was in season. There was a small vacant lot just across the street from our store and most of the time that's where we would play football or baseball or basketball. However, when we were needed in the store to deliver some groceries, our dad would step out on the front porch of the store and whistle. And Bob and I would hear that whistle and we would respond immediately and run to the store to do our job.

That was the covenant we had with Mom and Dad. "Go out and play and have fun, but when you hear Dad's whistle, stop what you are doing immediately, and come running to help out." The whistle meant "Come quickly! You are needed now! I've got a job for you!" This was the understanding we had and it was so strong that if we were in the midst of a baseball game and had just gotten a hit and we were rounding first base heading for second, and heard that whistle, we forgot about second base and we ran to do our job. If we were playing football and running for a touchdown, and heard that whistle, we would just run right through the end zone, toss the ball back to our friends, and run as fast as our legs could carry us to the store to do our job.

That's what it meant to be a part of our family: when we heard Dad's whistle, we knew to drop everything and come running because he needed us; he had a job for us.

If all of us will be real still and real quiet, and listen real closely, you know what we will hear? A whistle. Our Heavenly Father is whistling right now. He is whistling for you, and with that whistle he is saying, "Come quickly! You are needed now! I've got a job for you! I've got a job that only you can do in your special way!"

This is what this passage in Mark 1 is all about. Simon and Andrew and James and John were fishing one day, just doing what they did every day. But then along came Jesus and he said to them, "Come, follow me and I will make you fishers of people" (v. 17, author's paraphrase). And look what they did. They dropped everything and came running. Why? Because they heard that whistle; they heard the call. And please notice this: they were not ordained ministers. They were not professional clergy. They were not formally trained theologians. They were not Bible scholars. They were lay-people, fishermen, regular folks who were willing to respond and follow and serve. These were the people Jesus called to do his work, and in so doing, he shows us that the key is not the ability; it's the availability.

In his book *The Applause of Heaven,* Max Lucado reminds us that if God can use ordinary inanimate objects (just everyday things) to do his work, then he can use us. He recalls how God used the staff of Moses to lead the people of Israel to freedom, the stone of little David to turn back a giant, and the saliva of Jesus to heal a blind man.

He points out that when we freely offer to God what we have, whatever it may be, he can, through the miracle of his grace, make the mundane majestic, the dull divine, and the humdrum holy. He reminds us that when it comes to serving God, the key is not ability, but the availability.

And then he says this:

Blessed are the available . . . the conduits, the tunnels, the tools. Deliriously joyful are the ones who believe that if God has used sticks, rocks, and spit to do his will, then he can use us.

We would do well to learn a lesson from the rod, the rock, and the saliva. They didn't complain. They didn't question God's wisdom. They didn't suggest an alternative plan. Perhaps the reason [God] has used so many inanimate objects for his mission is that they don't tell him how to do his job!

It's like the story of the barber who became an artist. When asked why he changed professions, he replied, "A canvas doesn't tell me how to make it beautiful." (p. 74)

Neither do the available. They just hear the whistle; they just respond to the call and humbly offer themselves in obedience to God. "Here am I, Lord, send me. Here am I, Lord, use me. Here am I, Lord, give me a job."

A few years ago we at St. Luke's United Methodist Church decided to write a one-sentence mission statement for our church. We worked hard at that. How do we describe who we are as a church in one sentence? Well, after a lot of prayer and discussion and conversation, here's what we came up with: "St. Luke's is a Christ-centered servant church where every member has a ministry."

I love that because it reminded us that we are centered in Christ and that we are his servants as we try our best to continue his ministry of preaching, teaching, caring, helping, healing, and giving ourselves sacrificially. But also, that mission statement kept before us an urgent, important question, namely this: Have you found your ministry? Have you found your special place of service? Have you figured out yet just where God can use you in the church? Remember now, it's not the ability; it's the availability. If you will make yourself available, then God will take it from there.

FIRST, OUR SERVICE IS A SYMBOL OF OUR GRATITUDE

One of my favorite words in the English language is *thanksgiving* because that word describes well what it means to be a Christian. As Christians, when we give ourselves in service we are expressing our gratitude to God for what he has done for us in Jesus Christ. That's how we say "thank you" to him, by serving him and his church.

Let me show you what I mean. In Scotland there is a lighthouse called Old William's Light. The man who kept the light would come into town two times each week to get groceries and to go to church. But one day, he failed to show up at his regular time. There had been a bad storm the night before, so his friends were worried about him. They went over to the lighthouse and found him there on the floor by the light, unconscious.

He had slipped on the rocks and had broken his leg. But he knew that the light needed to be lit that night. So, in great pain and with incredible effort, he had agonizingly crawled up those long and steep spiral stairs to the top, in order to turn on the light. Amazingly, he did it. He got the light on and then collapsed on the floor.

Because of his weakened condition, he caught pneumonia and later died in the hospital. After his funeral, a man came and said, "I want to erect a monument to this light keeper. I was the captain of a ship and was caught in the storm that night. I did not know where I was and was headed for the rocks. But then suddenly, the light came on and I was able to see where I was, and steer the ship to safety. I am so grateful to that light keeper. He, by his sacrificial act, saved my life." Then the captain said, "This is the first time in my life I can truly say somebody died that I may live."

He was wrong, of course, because 2,000 years ago on a hill called Calvary, Christ died so that that captain could live. Christ preached love, he stood tall for what was right, and then he climbed up on a cross for you and me, to die that we might live!

How could we not be amazed by that? How could we not be grateful for that? He did all of that for you and me. The question is, What are we doing to show our gratitude to him?

SECOND, OUR SERVICE IS A SYMBOL OF OUR LOVE

The Bible clearly teaches us that we are called to be servants of love. Servants, not privileged people, not pampered people, not passive people, not holier-than-thou people, but servant people.

On page after page of the Bible, we hear the following commands: Serve! Love! Give yourself! Reach out to others with help and healing! Be God's servants! Sacrifice yourself! Continue Christ's ministry of compassion! We hear that theme all through the Scriptures, and yet deep down inside, we wonder:

- Does God really mean that?
- Does he really mean me?
- Does he want me to be a servant?
- Does he want me to sacrifice?

Well, he showed us he meant it, on a cross! But still, we have to admit the plain fact that much of our world turns a deaf ear to that biblical call. We see that vividly by the ways in which people view and perceive themselves today. Let me show you what I mean.

Philip Yancey a few years ago wrote a fascinating magazine article about personal fulfillment in life. He said that in his career as a writer and journalist, he had interviewed all kinds of people. He divides them into two groups: the stars and the servants.

Interestingly and strangely, Philip Yancey expresses sympathy for the Stars. These are people who are in the limelight and who receive a lot of recognition and a lot of applause. He feels sorry for them. So many of them, he says, are so unhappy. "These idols," he says, "are as miserable a group of people as I have ever met." He says that these superstars seem to have more personal problems, more troubled psyches, more incurable self-doubts than most other persons. His point is clear: the self-indulgent, self-centered, pampered lifestyle will not work; it is not fulfilling.

On the other hand, Yancey discovered that those people who see themselves not as stars but as servants are radiantly happy people. Relief workers in Bangladesh, mission workers in Costa Rica, church and community volunteers, PhDs scattered through the jungles of South America translating the Bible into obscure languages; in these he sees an indescribable joy and strength and serenity.

Then Yancey says a fascinating thing: "I was prepared to honor and admire these servants, to uphold them as inspiring examples, but what surprised me was that I found myself envying them!" He then concluded by saying, "As I now reflect on those two groups — the stars and the servants — the servants clearly emerge as the favored ones, the graced ones. They work for low pay, long hours, and no applause, giving away their talents in love among the poor and uneducated. But, somehow in the process of losing their lives for others, they have found them."

Does that sound at all familiar? It should! This is precisely what Jesus said 2,000 years ago: "If you will lose yourself reaching out to others in love, you will find yourself" (author's translation).

Now, let me ask you a question. Be honest now. How do you see yourself? Do you see yourself as a superstar? As one who wants and expects to be catered to and pampered? As one whose major interest in life is self-indulgence? Or do you see yourself as a sidelines spectator? As one who never really gets on the playing field, but rather is content to sit complacently on the sidelines and critique and criticize what others are trying to do? Or do you see yourself as a sacrificial servant? As one who hears God's call to service, and says, "Here am I Lord, send me! Use me! Make me the instrument of your love!"

You know what the Bible says about this, don't you? The Bible clearly calls us to be servants — sacrificial servants, self-giving servants — who reach out to help others in the spirit of Christlike love. We must never forget that, because service is the symbol of our gratitude and our love.

THIRD, OUR SERVICE IS A SYMBOL OF OUR COMMITMENT

He was a retired carpenter. He heard that his church was going to send clothes to an orphanage in China. He volunteered to build some crates for shipping the clothes. He worked at the church all day and really enjoyed it. However, when he got home, he realized that his brand-new eyeglasses were missing. They had fallen out of his shirt pocket into one of the crates, and his new glasses were heading for China!

It was the time of the Great Depression and he had that very morning spent $20 for those glasses. He was upset. "It's not fair!" he complained to God. "I give my time and talent and money to your work and now this."

Months later, the director of the orphanage came from China to the United States to thank the church. "Thank you so much for sending the clothing to our orphanage," he said. "The children were so excited and so grateful. But also," he said, "I must thank you for the glasses you sent. You see, the Communists had just swept through the orphanage, destroying everything, including my glasses. I was desperate. Even if I had the money, there was simply no way of replacing those glasses. Along with not being able to see well, I experience terrible headaches every day. So my coworkers and I were much in prayer about this. Then your crates arrived, and there on top of the clothes in the first crate we opened was this pair of glasses, and amazingly," he said, "when I tried on the glasses it was like they had been custom-made just for me! Thank you, thank you for your part in this great miracle!"

The church people listened, happy for the miracle of the glasses, but, silently, they were thinking, "He must have us mixed up with another church because we didn't send any glasses." But sitting quietly in the back of the room, with tears streaming down his face, an ordinary carpenter realized the Master Carpenter had used him in an extraordinary way.

That's how it works. When we find our ministry, our place of service, when we hear God's whistle and respond and do our best, then God will take it from there and do miraculous things. So go find your place of service because our service is a symbol of our gratitude, our love, our commitment.

CHAPTER NINE:
THE PRIORITY OF
GOD'S CHURCH

SCRIPTURE: ISAIAH 6:1–8

When our children, Jodi and Jeff, first went off to college, I did what any good dad would do. I gave each of them, in turn, some helpful fatherly advice. Would you believe I gave them three points of fatherly advice?

First, I said to them: "When you complete your bachelor's degree and your master's degree, then you can start dating."

They laughed at that and both of them promptly ignored that first piece of fatherly advice.

Second, I said to them: "You will be on the college campus for four years and during that time I would like for you to find one building on campus. It's called the library."

Now, let me digress to tell you something I have learned over the years: boys and girls are different.

When our daughter, Jodi, went off to college, her mother and I talked to her every day (and we still do). She called us or we called her every day. That's the way daughters are.

On the other hand, guys are different. When our son, Jeff, went off to college, he was playing football at the university, and living in the football players' dorm.

Days went by and weeks went by and no word from Jeff. He didn't call. And when we called him, we couldn't reach him. His sister was seeing him every day and she assured us that he was OK, but we wanted to hear his voice and be sure he was handling college life well.

Finally, I decided to call him at 11:30 at night. Surely, he would be in his room at 11:30 at night. I rang his room at 11:30 that night and a girl answered the phone. I said, "Oh, I'm sorry, I must have dialed the wrong number. I was trying to reach Jeff Moore's room in the football dorm."

She said, "This is Jeff Moore's room."

I said what any father would say in a moment like that: "Oh! . . . This is Jeff's dad. Is Jeff there?"

She said, "Oh, no, Mr. Moore, he's not here. He's in the library studying. He goes to the library to study every night."

Now, that's what you call "rising to the occasion." We found out later that the girl was Jeff's roommate's girlfriend. At least that's what we were told.

Now, the third piece of fatherly advice I gave our children as they went off to college was this: "You will be on your own with a new sense of freedom on the college campus, but don't get out of the habit of going to church."

With the first two pieces of fatherly advice I gave them, I was really joking and teasing with them and they knew that. But on this last one, "Don't get out of the habit of going to church," I was dead serious.

I used the word *habit* on purpose because the truth is, going to church is a habit and not going to church is a habit.

Over the years, we have called going to church a "Holy Habit" and that's exactly what it is. It is also a "Sacred Promise." All of us who are members of the church stood at the altar and promised God that we would support the church with our presence.

We promised God we would be here. We promised God that attending church regularly, faithfully, would be a top priority in our lives and in our schedules. We made that promise, and we reaffirm that vow every Sunday with every new member who joins our church.

One Saturday afternoon, I was watching a football game on television. Ohio State was playing Wisconsin in a rainstorm. It wasn't just sprinkling; it was raining hard, and there was not an empty seat in that stadium. Over 80,000 people sat there in the rain to watch that game and support their schools. I switched channels and the same thing was happening in Florida. Miami and Florida State were playing football in a rainstorm and the stadium was jam-packed. Over 80,000 people sat there in the hard, driving rain supporting their football teams.

Let me ask you something? Are you that loyal to your church? How are you doing really in your church attendance? How faithful are you?

Let me put that in perspective by asking you some questions:

- If your car would start one out of three times, would you consider it faithful?
- If your television worked 60 percent of the time, would you consider it faithful?
- If your newspaper delivery person should skip your house every other day and an occasional Friday, would you call that faithful?
- If your water heater should greet you

113

with cold water in your shower three mornings a week, would it be faithful?

- If you should fail to come to work five or six days each month, would your employer consider you faithful?
- If you should miss a couple of house payments in a year, would your mortgage holder say, "Oh, well, ten out of twelve months; that's not too bad!"
- If you attend church once or twice a month — 25 to 50 percent of the time — would you say that you're faithful?

It is something to think about, isn't it? Now, with all of this as a backdrop for our thinking, let me give you my list of three reasons why we go to church; three reasons for going to church faithfully that explode out of our Scripture in Isaiah 6. In this powerful and graphic story, we see the prophet Isaiah experiencing the presence of God in the Temple in a life-changing way, and out of that experience, he senses the importance of three dramatic things:

- a right relationship with God,
- a right respect for other people,
- and a right reason for living.

And that is precisely what worship does

for us. Let's take a look at these together, one at a time.

First, Going to Church Calls Us to a Right Relationship With God; It Draws Us Closer to God

Isaiah came to "church" that day, and he had one of those mountaintop experiences with God; an experience much too powerful to express in words; an experience that drew him closer than ever into a right relationship with God.

Put that over against this. Do you remember how in the New Testament right after the miracle of Easter, the risen Lord appeared to the disciples in the Upper Room and they were absolutely bowled over by this incredible experience of seeing with their own eyes the resurrected Christ. He had defeated sin and death, the most stunning, amazing miracle of all time, the greatest news of all time and together as a church family the disciples all experienced it — all, that is, except Thomas.

Thomas missed it for one reason and one reason only. He was not there! He was absent!

Now, we know in his grace and compassion, the risen Lord came back and appeared again later, just for Thomas. But it's

115

a haunting story, isn't it? There's a sermon there somewhere and I think it has to do with this: how many great moments with God have you missed? How many life-changing moments with God have you missed simply because you weren't there, simply because you were absent from church, simply because you haven't really made up your mind yet to really commit your life to God and the church?

There's a great story about Dr. Stuart Henry, professor emeritus at Duke University. He taught American Christianity there for many years. Dr. Henry was walking across the Duke campus one Sunday morning and the bells in the chapel tower were ringing loudly up ahead. He was dressed in his Sunday best and he was walking briskly as if not to be late for the opening of the service.

A student saw him and said, "Hi there, Dr. Henry. Did you decide that you would go to church this morning?"

Dr. Henry kept walking and said, "No, I didn't decide to do that this morning."

The student looked puzzled. "Oh, I'm sorry," the student said. "I could have sworn you were going to chapel."

"I am," Dr. Henry said, "but I didn't decide to go this morning."

The student, somewhat baffled, said, "Oh, I guess I don't understand."

And Dr. Henry replied, "Look, son, I didn't make the decision to go to church this morning. I made that decision more than fifty years ago when I first became a Christian. So, it is never a decision whether I'll go to church, but only a decision of where I'll go to church." (Norman Neaves, *Settle It Once and For All,* 10-30-94)

Isn't that great? Dr. Henry just settled it once and for all a long time ago. He said, "I'm a Christian, I go to church, and it makes my life happier and fuller and more exciting than ever before."

It's so simple, and it saves a lot of time and energy. Just make the decision one time. You don't have to grapple with that every week. "Do you go to church?" "Of course I do. I'm a Christian!"

Let me ask you something. Have you done that? Have you made that decision to trust God, and to put him and the church at the top of your priority list? Have you decided once and for all to support God and the church with your presence in worship every Sunday?

As Isaiah learned many years ago, going to church will draw us closer to God and will give us amazing spiritual strength. As someone said, "We don't keep the Sabbath; the Sabbath keeps us."

SECOND, GOING TO CHURCH CALLS US TO A RIGHT RESPECT FOR OTHER PEOPLE

In church that day, Isaiah became concerned about the people. He wanted to reach out and help them. Church at its best makes us more compassionate people.

Statistics show that people who go to church regularly are happier and more satisfied than those who don't. And regular churchgoers live longer, a new study has revealed. Think of that, going to church adds years to your life and life to your years.

Regular churchgoers, in my opinion, seem to be more loving, more generous, more caring, more gracious, more moral, more honest, more accepting of others. They are less prejudiced, more committed to family life, and more involved in working and serving out in the community to improve the quality of life for everybody, and especially for the less fortunate.

Why is that? It's because no institution in the world teaches love and compassion like the church does. Remember when someone asked Mother Teresa how she could find the strength to work daily with all those needy

118

people? She answered: "Every person is Christ for me, and since there is only one Jesus, that person is the one person in the world at that moment."

She learned that in church. The church teaches us to see every person we meet as Christ in disguise. The church teaches us that we are not isolated Christians. We are family.

One of my favorite poems says it well.

You cannot pray the Lord's Prayer and
　　even once say "I";
You cannot pray the Lord's Prayer and
　　even once say "My";
Nor can you pray the Lord's Prayer and
　　not pray for another,
For when you pray for daily bread you
　　must include your brother
For others are included in each and every
　　plea;
From the beginning to the end of it,
It does not once say "Me."

THIRD, GOING TO CHURCH CALLS US TO A RIGHT REASON FOR LIVING, TO MINISTRY, AND TO SERVE

Isaiah, too, was given a reason for living, for ministry, and a call to serve that day long ago. There in church, he felt the tug of God.

He realized that a prophet was needed for that time. And, he said, "Here am I; send me!"

Let me ask you to picture something in your minds with me. Imagine, if you will, that you are watching the Super Bowl. The teams are introduced, and everybody stands for the national anthem. Then each team huddles up on their respective sidelines with their coaches. Suddenly, the referee blows his whistle to start the game.

Now, what would you think if, at that moment, all of those talented football players, the starting teams for both sides, stayed on the sidelines, and the coaches ran out onto the field to play the game? Pro-Bowl standouts, superstars, and the league's best players all stay on the sidelines while the coaching staff takes the field.

The players, on their sidelines, shout encouragement to their coaches — "Go get 'em, Coach!" "You can do it, Coach!" "We're all behind you, Coach!" — but none of the players go out on the playing field. They expect the coaches to do it all.

If you saw that happen at the game, what would you think? You would probably think, "This is the most bizarre thing I've ever seen. Look at all those talented players standing there. Why aren't they putting on their helmets and taking the field? Why are they staying on the sidelines and watching their coaches play the game? This is crazy!"

And yet, that's the way some people relate to the church. They think the ordained ministers and staff are supposed to do it all, while they stand by and watch. But that is certainly not biblical.

Think about it. Jesus did not call a single priest or rabbi to be one of his disciples. He called laypeople to help him do his work! And he is calling you right now. He has a special job that only you can do.

Can you hear his call? And can you say with Isaiah: "Here am I; send me!"

Going to church, supporting the church with our presence; that is so important because it draws us closer to God. It gives us compassion for others and it calls us to ministry.

Going to church; it is so important because it calls us to a right relationship with God, a right respect for others, and a right reason for living. And that's why church is a great priority for our lives.

CHAPTER TEN:
THE PRIORITY OF BEING A MIRACLE WORKER FOR GOD

SCRIPTURE: ACTS 3:1–10

Some time ago, I saw a miracle of love on Larchmont Street. I was driving down Larchmont on the way to church. On the sidewalk near me was a young woman, probably in her twenties. All of a sudden a huge ferocious-looking dog came over a fence barking, growling, snarling, and charging right toward the young woman.

Now what do you think the young woman did? Run away? Faint? Burst into tears? Climb a tree? Jump into my car? Scream for help? No. None of these. Rather, she ran straight at the dog; she challenged him; she stared him down; she turned him back; she ran him off; and then she continued her morning walk.

Now, what was it that made her so courageous? What was it that enabled her to stare danger in the face with such boldness? Let me tell you, it was love! For, you see, she was not alone that morning. She was pushing her baby in a stroller. And when the barking, snarling dog started toward them, she did what any mother would do. She positioned herself between the dog and her baby. She was more concerned about her baby's safety than her own safety. She was more concerned about her baby's welfare than her own welfare. Her love made her brave and bold and courageous.

Later, when her husband heard what she had done he called it a miracle of love because he knew that all of her life, she had been terrified of dogs, morbidly afraid of dogs. Her husband was right. It was indeed a miracle of love.

The Bible is full of "love miracles" like that. When Jesus healed Bartimaeus, who was blind, it was a miracle of love. When Jesus converted Zacchaeus, it was a miracle of love. When he went to the cross for you and me, it was a miracle of love. When he came out of the tomb, it was a miracle of love.

And that's what we see here in this Scripture lesson for today. Look at it with me: Acts 3:1–10. Here we see the miraculous healing of the man at the Beautiful Gate of the Temple. It was indeed a miracle of love.

In the musical *Go Out Singing,* this story is one of the most wonderful scenes in the play. Here is the context: Pentecost has just happened. The Holy Spirit has come. And now Peter and John are going up to the Temple when they see this man who cannot walk and is having to beg, and in the play a conversation takes place in which John encourages Peter to try to heal the man. Peter is hesitant understandably. Who is he to think that he could perform a miracle? How presumptuous! But, John persists. John reminds him of the Lord's promise to be with them. Peter protests again, saying he has no power to heal, no power to perform miracles. But John will not be put off and points out that it won't hurt to give it a try. Nothing ventured, nothing gained. Finally, although quite reluctantly, with fear and trembling and with not much confidence, Peter walks over to the beggar and with great hesitancy, he stammers, "Um . . . uh . . . ummm . . . oh . . . in the name of Jesus Christ of Nazareth, I . . . uh . . . I . . . uh bid you rise and walk." The beggar stares at Peter as if Peter is crazy. Peter stares back with diminishing hope. Finally, Peter breaks, turns, and walks downstage. Peter looks up toward the heavens with great embarrassment and begins to fervently pray for forgiveness, admitting that he has overstepped his bounds, confessing that it was a stupid and arrogant and foolish thing for him to even think that he could perform a miracle and heal the lame man. On and on Peter goes begging for forgiveness.

Now while Peter is saying all of that, behind him, the beggar is getting up on his feet, brushing himself off, testing his legs and suddenly he is shouting for everyone to look at him and see how (miraculously, incredibly) he can walk! Instantly confident, Peter looks back at him and says: "Of course you can." Then in the musical, Peter and the healed man break into a magnificent song-and-dance soft-shoe routine called, "Praise, Praise the Lord," with the healed man dancing all over the stage, bringing down the house. At the conclusion of that number, people are amazed, and they are congratulating the healed man on how well he can walk now and what an unbelievable miracle this is: him walking! And the healed man tells them that there is something even more wondrous and even more marvelous. What's that? they ask him. The man answers that he didn't know he could dance!

This is a serendipity. The beggar was looking for alms, for money, and he got something different, something better. "I have no silver and gold, but I give you what I have; in the name of Jesus Christ of Nazareth, rise and walk." And the man does!

Now, this is one of the most fascinating love miracles of the Scriptures because it not only records the healing of this man but it also suggests that we, too, through the grace of God, can be miracle workers. Jesus put it strongly in the Gospel of John (14:12) when he said, "Truly I say to you, those who believe in me will also do the works that I do and greater works than these will you do" (author's translation).

Let me ask you a question. If you had the power right now to perform one miracle, what would it be? What would you do? The way we would answer that question would reveal a lot about us, wouldn't it? Now, with that as a backdrop, let's look together at three possibilities for you and me today.

First, We Can (With the Help of God) Be Miracle Workers With Our Words

Words are so powerful. They can build up or, sadly, they can tear down. Recently, I have been thinking about my own life, and wondering what in the world would have happened to me had it not been for certain people who came along to give me just the right words at just the right time; words that turned my life around, words that picked me up when I was down, words that gave me new life.

I remember my first sermon, preached at St. Mark's Methodist Church in Memphis. I was a tenth grader, sixteen years old. I got up in the pulpit, read the Scripture lesson, preached all the way from Genesis to Revelation, and drank three glasses of water in four minutes! Four minutes and it was over! Now, I know some people like four-minute sermons, but I felt awful — embarrassed, defeated, humiliated, ashamed — and during that last hymn I thought, "This is not for me. I can't do this. I'll never try this again." But then after the service, one of the older saints of the church came up and shook my hand and with a warm smile he said, "Son, you just did fine! You did really well. I'm so proud of you. I think you've got the makings of a minister, and I believe God's gonna make a preacher out of you."

Now, as I think back on that moment, I know that he was probably just feeling sorry for me, but I will always be grateful to him for giving me the right words at the right time. It was a miracle what those words did for me. Those words picked me up, lifted me up, inspired me, and made me want to try again. We can work love-miracles for one another with our words.

SECOND, WE CAN (WITH THE HELP OF GOD) BE MIRACLE WORKERS WITH OUR ATTITUDES

I have seen it many times. The attitude of one person can change the whole atmosphere of a place. An office, a class, a neighborhood, a church, a family; the whole situation can be changed, redeemed, made better by the influence of one person.

Some time ago, we helped a young woman in our church get a job. After she had been in that new position for about a month, her boss called to take me to lunch and he said, "I want to talk to you about that young woman you sent to us last month." I was worried and said, "Is she not working out?" And he said, "Oh, no, just the opposite. She is great! And I wanted to tell you she has absolutely worked a miracle in my office. The whole attitude has changed. She is a ray of sunshine. It is unbelievable what she has done and I wanted to thank you for sending her to us." We can be miracle workers with our words and with our attitudes.

Third, We Can (With the Help of God) Be Miracle Workers With Our Actions

In the spring of 1887, Helen Keller, who was deaf and blind, seemed terrifying to those around her. She uttered unintelligible animal sounds and in a rage would smash dishes and throw herself on the floor in frightening temper tantrums. The conclusion of many persons was that Helen's situation was hopeless, and there wasn't much reason to doubt that conclusion.

But then along came Anne Sullivan into little Helen's life. Anne Sullivan, a twenty-year-old tutor, arrived at the Keller home in Tuscumbia, Alabama, to be Helen Keller's teacher. For weeks and weeks, she got nowhere. She tried and tried to break through by spelling words into Helen's hands, but with no luck. Finally, on April 5, a breakthrough occurred. At the well house, Helen was holding a mug under a spout. Anne Sullivan pumped water into the mug and when the water poured onto Helen's hand, she continued to spell w-a-t-e-r into Helen's other hand. Suddenly, Helen understood! The lightbulb turned on! She grabbed Anne's ever-ready hand and begged her for more words. A new world had opened for Helen Keller, and she flourished in it.

Anne Sullivan spent most of her life with Helen Keller. She went to college with Helen, sitting by her throughout every class at Radcliff. Helen went on to become the friend of kings and princes, and an inspiration to the whole world. All because of the actions of a young twenty-year-old teacher who would not quit, who would not give up, and who kept on loving and caring for Helen Keller when it seemed so hopeless. Don't miss this now. Later, when they wrote a play about Anne Sullivan's work with Helen Keller, do you remember what they called it? That's right: *The Miracle Worker.* A perfect title, because her actions with God's help worked a miracle. We can be miracle workers with our words, our attitudes, and our actions.

Please notice this. When Peter healed the man in Acts 3, he did it "in the name of Jesus Christ." "In the name of Jesus Christ of Nazareth, stand up and walk," he said (v. 6). Now, that phrase, "in the name of Jesus," means "in the spirit of Jesus." And the message is clear: when we act in the name of Jesus Christ, when we live in the spirit of Jesus Christ, we can do incredible, amazing things. When we live in the spirit of Christ, we can be miracle workers with our words, our attitudes, and our actions.

CHAPTER ELEVEN: THE PRIORITY OF HAVING A STRONG CASE OF THE "CAN'T HELP IT"S

SCRIPTURE: JOHN 1:35–42

One of the great celebrative anthems is the powerful African American spiritual "Ain't Got Time to Die." It was written by Hall Johnson, and it has these joyfully dramatic words: "Been so busy serving my Master . . . / Ain't got time to die."

In this inspiring and wonderful spiritual, the composer is underscoring and celebrating the joy and excitement of being a Christian, the joy and excitement of serving our Lord in gratitude for what he has done for us.

The point that this spiritual is trying to drive home to us with great enthusiasm is that when we really become Christians, when we really commit our lives to Christ, we can't sit still. We become so excited, so thrilled, so grateful for our new life in Christ that we can't help loving him, praising him, serving him, and sharing him with others.

This is precisely what happened to Andrew. He found the Messiah, he encountered Jesus, and he was so excited he couldn't sit still. Immediately, gratefully, excitedly, he ran to share the good news with his brother Simon. It reads like this in the first chapter of John's Gospel: "[Andrew] first found his brother Simon and said to him, 'We have found the Messiah' " (v. 41).

Then Andrew brought Simon Peter to Jesus. This was the greatness of Andrew. He was the man who was always introducing others to Jesus. Three different times in the Bible, Andrew comes to center stage, and each time he is bringing someone to meet Jesus.

Here in John 1, he brings his brother Simon Peter. In John 6, Andrew brings to Jesus the boy with the five loaves and two fish. And in John 12, we find Andrew, along with Philip, bringing to Jesus the inquiring Greeks who wanted to meet Jesus and visit with him.

Andrew's greatest joy was sharing the good news of Christ and bringing others into the presence of Christ. Having found Jesus, he could not sit still, he could not help it. He had to share Christ with others.

An ordained minister friend of mine tells

about a woman in his church who is so excited to be a Christian. She had a troubled past and had pretty much hit bottom when a friend reached out to her and brought her to church. The church members welcomed her warmly and loved her into the circle of their love and God's love. She started going to church faithfully. She joined a wonderful Sunday school class. She began studying the Bible daily. She started praying regularly, and in the process was converted. She realized for the very first time in her life that God loved her, even her! She came to understand that even though she had done all those sordid things in her earlier life that God still loved her, forgave her, accepted her, valued her, treasured her. She was absolutely bowled over by that "amazing grace" and she committed herself to Christ, heart and soul. Recently, she said to her pastor, "I'm so excited to be a Christian, that I've got a strong case of the 'can't help it's.'"

This is also true of Andrew. He, too, had a strong case of the "can't help it"s. He was so grateful, so thrilled, so excited about Christ that he just could not sit still. *He could not keep Jesus to himself.* You know, as I think about this, and as I think about my own personal life and spiritual pilgrimage, I can tell you that I also have a strong case of the "can't help it"s. It goes with being a Christian. Let me show you what I mean by speaking out of my own personal life with three thoughts. Try these on for size with me, and I'm sure that you will think of others out of your own personal and spiritual life, but for now, let me share these three with you.

FIRST, BECAUSE WE ARE CHRISTIANS, WE CAN'T HELP BEING GRATEFUL

Andrew, along with the people of his time, was longing for a Messiah to come, hoping for a Messiah, praying for a Messiah. When he found the Messiah in Jesus, he was incredibly grateful.

You know, there is no such thing as an ungrateful Christian. Christianity by definition is our grateful response to God for his love of the world and his gift to the world of Jesus Christ. Responsive gratitude. That's what Christianity is all about.

A group of young students was asked by their schoolteacher to make a list of what they thought were the present-day Seven Wonders of the World. Although there were some disagreements, the following seven things received the most votes:

1. The Great Pyramids of Egypt
2. The Taj Mahal
3. The Grand Canyon
4. The Panama Canal
5. The Empire State Building
6. St. Peter's Basilica
7. China's Great Wall

While gathering the votes, the teacher noted that one quiet student had not turned in her paper yet. So she asked the girl if she was having trouble with her list. The girl replied, "Yes, a little. I couldn't quite make up my mind because there were so many."

The teacher said, "Well, tell us what you have. Read your list and maybe we can help."

Hesitantly, shyly, the girl stood up and then read her paper out loud to the class. She said, "I think the Seven Wonders of the World are:

1. to be able to see
2. to be able to hear
3. to be able to touch
4. to be able to feel
5. to be able to taste
6. to be able to laugh
7. to be able to love."

The room was so quiet when she finished

that you could have heard a pin drop. Isn't it amazing how we overlook and take for granted the gifts that God has given us? We become so captivated by man-made things that we sometimes forget the astounding generosity of God.

The psalmist did not make that mistake. Read the psalms. They resound on page after page with praise and gratitude to God. Psalm 100 is a classic example:

Make a joyful noise to the LORD, all the
  earth.
Worship the LORD with gladness;
  come into his presence with singing.

Know that the LORD is God.
  It is he that made us, and we are his;
  we are his people, and the sheep of his
  pasture.

Enter his gates with thanksgiving,
  and his courts with praise.
  Give thanks to him, bless his name.

For the LORD is good;
  his steadfast love endures forever,
  and his faithfulness to all generations.

This is just a sample of how the psalms

reverberate with gratitude. That same theme of praise and gratitude is still very much in evidence in our present-day hymnals. Hymns like "How Great Thou Art"; "Now Thank We All Our God"; "Come, Ye Thankful People, Come"; "Sing Praise to God Who Reigns Above"; "O For a Thousand Tongues to Sing"; "Joyful, Joyful We Adore Thee"; and hundreds more like these great hymns of gratitude fill our hymnals and our hearts.

Why? Because the great theme of our Christian faith, hope and love, is the spirit of gratitude — gratitude for God's presence with us, for God's watchcare over us, for God's forgiveness of us, for God's salvation for us.

A missionary in Africa was preaching his first sermon in a mission church. When the time came for the offering, the people danced their offerings forward. They danced and sang praise to God as they brought their offerings to the altar. It was a beautiful moment.

After the service, he asked one of the people, "Why do you dance and sing when you bring your offering forward on Sunday morning?"

Back came the answer: "How could we not dance? We are so grateful to God for what he has done for us in sending Jesus Christ to save us that we have to dance and sing our thanksgiving. And besides, it says in the Bible, God loves a cheerful giver."

Let me ask you something. Do you feel gratitude to God that strongly? Do you have a strong case of the "can't help it"s when it comes to gratitude? When you are a Christian, gratitude is the spirit of your lifestyle.

SECOND, BECAUSE WE ARE CHRISTIANS WE CAN'T HELP BEING CONFIDENT

Confidence is why Andrew kept bringing people to Christ; he had confidence in the Lord. Things were not always perfect, times and situations were sometimes hard, but Andrew never lost his confidence in Christ. He just did his best and then trusted God to bring it out right.

Someone once asked the great Christian Phillips Brooks why he seemed always to be so serene, poised, optimistic, and confident. I love Brooks's answer. He said simply, "I am a Christian."

A father and daughter were in their last moments together at the airport. The airline had announced the daughter's departure, and standing there near the security gate, they hugged and her father said, "I love you, and I wish you enough."

She replied, "Dad, our life together has been more than enough. Your love is all I ever needed. I love you so much, and I wish *you* enough, *too,* Dad." They hugged and held each other tightly and then she turned and left. The father walked over toward the window to watch his daughter's plane take off. Tears rolled down his cheeks.

Another man had been watching them. The father turned to the man and said, "Did you ever say good-bye to someone knowing that you would not see each other again in this lifetime?"

"Yes, I have," the man said. "Please forgive me for asking, but why is this a final good-bye?"

The father answered, "I am old now . . . not in good health and the real truth is that her next trip back will be for my funeral."

"I'm sorry," said the stranger.

"It's OK. I have had a wonderful life, and it will soon be over for me. But it's been a great ride. God has blessed me and he has always been with me, and he will be with me in the life to come. I have no regrets. I trust God for whatever is ahead."

The other man said, "May I ask you about something? When you were saying good-bye, I heard you say, 'I wish you enough.'

What does that mean?"

The father smiled and said, "That's a wish that has been handed down for many generations in my family. My parents used to say it to everyone."

When we say, "I wish you enough," we are wanting the other person to have enough good things to sustain them. The wish goes like this:

I wish you enough sun to keep your attitude bright.

I wish you enough rain to appreciate the sun more.

I wish you enough happiness to keep your spirit alive.

I wish you enough adversity so the smallest joys in life appear much bigger.

I wish you enough gain to satisfy your wanting.

I wish you enough loss to be grateful for all you possess.

I wish you enough hellos to get you through the final good-byes.

The father looked at the other man and said, "I wish you enough," and then he turned and walked away.

When we are Christians, we can be confident because in Christ, God gives us enough

140

— enough strength to keep us going, enough forgiveness to make us a new creation, enough courage to enable us to stand tall when times are tough, enough assurance to convince us that ultimately God wins and he wants to share his victory with us.

This is the good news. Nothing can separate us from God's love and watchcare. Nothing. Not trouble or pain or heartache or disappointment; not even death can cut us off from God and his love. God is always with us. That is God's promise. So, because we are Christians, we can be grateful, and we can be confident.

THIRD, BECAUSE WE ARE CHRISTIANS, WE CAN'T HELP BEING LOVING

Again, Andrew is a great example of love. He was bighearted, magnanimous, generous. He was a loving, caring person who was eager to share and eager to help others. If only we could learn that lesson from Andrew, life would be better for all of us.

Donna is a member of our church. She is a mentor in our Kids Hope USA program. Every week she goes to a nearby elementary school to be a friend, encourager, and mentor to a little boy named John. John looks to be six or seven years old. Donna and John have bonded in a beautiful way. Though there is quite a difference in their ages, Miss Donna — as John calls her — has become John's best friend. Once each week, she visits him at school, helps him with his school work, and then, "going the second mile" every Saturday, Donna takes John to do exciting things that without Donna, John would likely never get to do — things like going to the zoo, the museum, the mall.

A few months ago, Donna's husband died in his sleep. Little John came to the funeral to support his friend Miss Donna in her grief. At the reception after the memorial service, John stood beside Donna and held her hand. She had been there for him, and now he was there for her. He would not leave her side. It was a beautiful moment, and people in the room had tears in their eyes, so touched by John's intense commitment to lovingly stand by Miss Donna, his friend and mentor.

Some of us saw John eyeing the goodies on the reception table — punch and chocolate chip cookies in abundance — and some of us said to him, "John, would you like to walk over here and have some refreshments?" But no, he would not leave Donna's side.

"I want to stay here with Miss Donna," he would say. The love between the two of them was so radiant and powerful in that room.

Also in the room that day was a man from Chicago. He had flown all the way to Houston to be with Donna. Do you know why? Because thirty-eight years ago when he was in first grade, Donna had been his mentor at an elementary school in the Chicago area. He flies from Chicago to Houston every summer to see Donna and to thank her for what she did for him thirty-eight years ago — and then he made this special trip to be with Donna when her husband suddenly died. That man from Chicago says to Donna every time he comes, "I am what I am today because of the love and support you gave me thirty-eight years ago. Ms. Donna, you were the first person in my life who believed in me." And today little John says to her in words and actions: "Miss Donna, I love you. I know you love me. You are my best friend."

Now, where did Donna learn to love like that, to reach out to people in need like that, to make a difference in people's lives like that? You know, don't you? The same place the disciple Andrew learned it: from Jesus. You see, when you are a Christian, you get a strong case of the "can't help it"s. You can't help being grateful, you can't help being confident, you can't help being loving.

Chapter Twelve:
The Priority of
Prioritizing
SCRIPTURE: MATTHEW 5:30

Let me remind you of something they do in a certain village in Italy. They have a unique custom on New Year's Eve. They don't dress up and go to a festive party. They don't sing "Auld Lang Syne." They don't gather in the town square and watch a glittering ball drop to announce the exact moment when the new year begins. No, they pretty much all stay home, and as midnight approaches, traffic on the streets begins to lessen. Soon there is no traffic at all. No cars. No pedestrians. Even the police take cover because they know what's about to happen.

Then at the precise stroke of midnight the windows of every house in the village open up, and to the sound of music, fireworks, and laughter, people with reckless abandon begin to throw things out the windows. Things such as

- worn-out furniture,

144

- chipped glasses,
- cracked dishes,
- clothes gone out of style,
- old pots and pans they no longer want,
- old shoes that no longer fit,
- pictures of old boyfriends or girl-friends,
- personal items that remind them of difficult experiences in the past year.

Out the window they go. All those things that they do not want to carry with them into the new year go flying out the windows.

Actually, if you stop to think about it, the Italians in that little village have a great idea. Now if you decide to try this, and especially if you live in a high-rise, you may want to warn your neighbors that you're starting a new custom, and you may want to get permission from city hall, and your land-lord.

The point of this unique village custom, however, is well taken, because there are indeed times in our lives when we need to make a clean sweep of it. There are times in our lives when we need to stop and evaluate and throw out those things that are burdening us, hampering us, hurting us, and hurting those around us.

This is precisely what Jesus was talking

about in the Sermon on the Mount in Matthew 5 when he said those words that at first hearing seem so harsh and shocking: "And if your right hand causes you to sin, cut it off and throw it away" (v. 30*a*). *Cut it off and throw it away?* These words sound so strong, so stark, so startling. There must be some truth here that is tremendously important to prompt Jesus to speak so boldly and so unflinchingly. What are we to make of this?

Of course, we know that Jesus was speaking symbolically here. The actual literal cutting off of a hand was certainly not what Jesus had in mind at all. Jesus is speaking dramatically and symbolically here, calling us to the discovery of a much deeper truth, namely this: if you have something in your life right now that is destructive, then cut it out and throw it away! Get rid of it before it destroys you.

If you are smoking and destroying your lungs, quit smoking! If you are drinking and you are becoming an alcoholic, quit drinking! If you are gambling and losing all of your food money at the track, quit gambling! Whatever you are doing that is bad for you, and bad for those around you, cut it off, quit it, throw it out before it does you in.

Nowhere is this "cut it off and throw it

away" principle more true than in our spiritual lives. There are certain acts, certain attitudes, certain habits, certain sins that will contaminate, infest, and poison our souls. Jesus knew that, and he knew that the only way we can be spiritually fit and spiritually whole is to get rid of these acts, attitudes, habits, and sins.

Now, let me list three things we would do well to cut out of our lives and throw away.

FIRST, THROW OUT SELFISHNESS

If you read the Bible closely, you will discover that the real culprit in our spiritual lives is selfishness; and on the flip side of the coin, the height of spiritual maturity according to the Scriptures is love for God, and love for others.

I had a seminary professor who stated it strongly. He said there is really only one sin with a capital letter, with lots of little sins underneath. He said the big sin is the sin of idolatry, the worshiping of something other than God, and he said that something we most often put in front of God is "self." My professor went on to say that the sin of self-centeredness has much variation like pride, arrogance, immorality, prejudice, hatefulness, violence, stealing, hurting, and obscenity, but he said they are rooted to selfish-

147

ness. They all are rooted to putting self before God and before others.

This problem of selfishness is so threatening and so dangerous that Jesus used dramatic language to describe how we need to be converted from selfishness to love. He said, "We must be born again! We must die to selfishness before we can come alive to love" (author's paraphrase). Bishop Kenneth Shamblin once said, "Conversion means moving from 'That belongs to me' to 'I belong to that!'"

The noted psychologist Dr. Alfred Adler once put an ad in the newspaper that read, "Guaranteed: fourteen-day cure for loneliness." A woman showed up at his office, ad in hand, and said, "It says here that you can cure my loneliness in fourteen days. Is that true?"

"Absolutely," said Dr. Adler. "If you will do exactly what I tell you to do for fourteen days, you won't be lonely anymore."

"Tell me more," said the woman.

Dr. Adler said, "For fourteen consecutive days, I want you to go out and do something kind for somebody else."

The woman said, "Why should I do something kind for somebody else?" To which Dr. Adler said, "In your case, it might take twenty-one days."

When we live in the spirit of selfishness, we are likely to end up bitter and miserable or lonely. On the other hand, when we live as God meant for us to live, reaching out to others in the gracious, loving, thoughtful spirit of Christ, we will end up filled with a sense of meaning and purpose and joy and fulfillment.

An old Native American of the Cherokee tribe was telling his grandson about a battle that is going on inside himself, a battle between two wolves. One wolf is evil, representing anger, envy, greed, arrogance, self-pity, guilt, resentment, false pride, and ego. The other wolf is good, representing joy, peace, love, hope, humility, faith, benevolence, generosity, compassion, and kindness. The grandson thought about it for a minute and then asked his grandfather, "Which wolf wins?" The old Cherokee simply replied, "The one I feed."

Precisely so! And this is why Jesus taught us in words and deeds to feed and nurture love and kindness in our lives. This is why he told us over and over again to "Get rid of selfishness! Cut selfishness out of your life! You don't need it anymore! Cast it off! Throw it out!"

SECOND, THROW OUT DEFEAT

The Scriptures boldly and confidently tell us that if we put our faith and trust in God and commit our lives to him that we can't be defeated. Of course we will have some setbacks in life. Of course we will have some disappointments. Of course we will have some heartache and sorrow and pain, but the bottom line is God ultimately wins, and if we hang in there and count on God and trust in him, nothing, not even death, can defeat us. That is the great promise of the Bible.

Some years ago a young man named Bobby Burnett went to the University of Arkansas on a football scholarship. The coaches knew that he had been an outstanding running back in high school, but early on, they got the impression that Burnett was a fast runner, but that he didn't like to be hit. So, they used him like a tackling dummy. The veteran players hit him and hit him and hit him, working on their tackling techniques. Burnett never complained. He just kept getting back up. He refused to quit.

For three-and-a-half years, Burnett showed up for practice at the university, and he never dressed out for a game. Finally, they let him put on a uniform and stand on the sidelines. The coaches had no intention of putting him in the game. He had been the tackling dummy for three-and-a-half years and had never really had the chance to show what he could do in a football game.

But then that Saturday afternoon the first-string tailback got hurt and then the second-string tailback got hurt, and the coaches had no other choice than to reluctantly send Burnett into the game. On his first play in the game, they gave him the ball. He went through the hole, ran right over the line-backer, and made an outstanding run. From that point on, he was Arkansas's starting tailback, and he became a big-time star.

In the 1965 Cotton Bowl, Burnett made the key play that put Arkansas in a position to win the game. Two plays later, Burnett dived over the goal line, and Arkansas won the Cotton Bowl Game 10 to 7 against Nebraska, and the next day Arkansas was proclaimed National Champion.

The next year Burnett started every game, had a great season, made the All-Conference team, was drafted to play in the AFL, and in his first year as a pro was named "AFL Rookie of the Year." For three-and-a-half years at Arkansas, he didn't even dress out for the games, but he would not quit, he would not give up, he would not accept defeat.

If you do a study of the great champions in sports and in all aspects of life, you will find that they all have one common quality. It's not speed. It's not talent. It's not size. It is *persistence.* They will not quit. They will not give up. They will not accept defeat. They persist. They persevere. This is also the quality of the spiritual champions. They know God will ultimately win, and so they hang in there with God. They keep on trusting God, come what may.

So, as we move ahead into a new year or a new day, we can throw out the spirit of selfishness and we can throw out the spirit of defeat.

THIRD, THROW OUT ILL WILL

"Ill will." That's a phrase that means a lot of things and covers a multitude of sins. Bad temper, hostility, vengeance, resentment, arrogance, spite, hatefulness — all of these are what we mean by "ill will." And ill will is a fitting name for all of these because they are all sick. Nothing is more spiritually poisonous than ill will.

Christ came to bring us wholeness, to make us well, to deliver us from all these sins of ill will. Again, this is what conversion is. It is Christ coming into our lives and changing our "ill will" to "good will."

Have you heard about the man who was sitting in his car at a traffic light? He was second in line. When the light turned green, the car in front of him didn't go immediately, and the man in the second car went ballistic. He just lost it. He shouted expletives out the window. He honked his horn in a wild rage. He made obscene gestures toward the driver in front of him. Finally, the first car moved on through the intersection. The man in the second car made it through also, but he was still shouting and gesturing his profanities.

A police car pulled him over. The policeman got him out of the car, handcuffed him and searched him, and put him in the backseat of the squad car. The policeman called headquarters, talked for a few minutes, and then he helped the arrested man out of the backseat, took off the cuffs, and told the man he was free to go. The policeman said, "Well, surprise to me, it *is* your car, after all! Sorry for the inconvenience. You are free to go."

The baffled motorist asked, "What on earth was that all about?"

"Well," said the policeman, "when I saw the bumper stickers on the car that said, 'Honk if you love Jesus' and 'God loves you, and I love you,' and then I saw how you were acting, I just naturally assumed that you must have stolen that car!"

Well, the point is clear. Ill will is not representative of who we are as Christians, and we don't need to carry it around any longer. So now is a good time to throw some destructive things out of the window of our lives. It's a good time to throw out selfishness, to throw out defeat, and to throw out ill will, or in other words to invite God to take over the driver's seat in our lives.

DISCUSSION GUIDE

FOR JAMES W. MOORE'S *If God Is Your Co-Pilot, Swap Seats!*
JOHN D. SCHROEDER

This book by James W. Moore focuses on the importance of priorities and how important it is to make God the number-one priority in our lives.

This study guide was created to help make this experience beneficial for both you and members of your group. Here are some thoughts to assist you in facilitating a discussion group:

1. Distribute the book to participants before your first meeting and request that they come having read the first chapter. You may want to limit the size of your group to increase participation.

2. Begin your sessions on time. Your participants will appreciate your promptness. You may wish to begin your first session with introductions and a brief get-acquainted time. Start each session by reading aloud the snapshot summary of the

chapter for the day.

3. Select discussion questions and activities in advance. Note that the first question is a general question designed to get discussion going. The last question is designed to summarize the discussion. Feel free to change the order of the listed questions and to create your own questions. Allow a set amount of time for the questions and activities.

4. Remind participants that all questions are valid as part of the learning process. Encourage their participation in discussion by saying that there are no "wrong" answers and that all input will be appreciated. Invite participants to share their thoughts, personal stories, and ideas as their comfort level allows.

5. Some questions may be more difficult to answer than others. If you ask a question and no one responds, begin the discussion by venturing an answer yourself. Then ask for comments and other answers. Remember that some questions may have multiple answers.

6. Ask the questions "Why?" or "Why do you believe that?" to help continue a discussion and give it greater depth.

7. Give everyone a chance to talk. Keep the conversation moving. Occasionally you

may want to direct a question to a specific person who has been quiet. "Do you have anything to add?" is a good follow-up question to ask another person. If the topic of conversation gets off track, move ahead by asking the next question in your study guide.

8. Before moving from questions to activities, ask group members if they have any questions that have not been answered. Remember that as a leader, you do not have to know all the answers. Some answers may come from group members. Other answers may even need a bit of research. Your job is to keep the discussion moving and to encourage participation.

9. Review the activity in advance. Feel free to modify it or to create your own activity. Encourage participants to try the *At home* activity.

10. Following the conclusion of the activity, close with a brief prayer, praying either the printed prayer from the study guide or a prayer of your own. If your group desires, pause for individual prayer petitions.

11. Be grateful and supportive. Thank group members for their ideas and participation.

12. You are not expected to be a "perfect" leader. Just do the best you can by focusing

on the participants and the lesson. God will help you lead this group.

13. Enjoy your time together!

SUGGESTIONS FOR PARTICIPANTS

1. What you will receive from this study will be in direct proportion to your involvement. Be an active participant!

2. Please make a point to attend all sessions and to arrive on time so that you can receive the greatest benefit.

3. Read the chapter and review the study-guide questions prior to the meeting. You may want to jot down questions you have from the reading and also answers to some of the study-guide questions.

4. Be supportive and appreciative of your group leader as well as the other members of your group. You are on a journey together.

5. Your participation is encouraged. Feel free to share your thoughts about the material being discussed.

6. Pray for your group and your leader.

CHAPTER 1
If God Is Your Co-Pilot, Swap Seats!

Snapshot Summary

This chapter examines three keys to life. These include seeking God's will, obeying God's Word, and living God's way.

Reflection/Discussion Questions

1. Share your interest in reading and discussing this book. What do you hope to gain?

2. Describe a time when you needed God in the driver's seat of your life.

3. Give reasons why some people prefer God as their co-pilot rather than their pilot.

4. Why might some people be afraid that religion takes life away?

5. Reflect on/discuss how religion and faith enhance your life and add value to it.

6. Name some ways to seek God's will. How do you know what God wants you to do?

7. Reflect on/discuss the purposes of the Bible. How does the Bible help us obey God's Word?

8. Name some ways to reach out to others in love and to help those in need.

9. What does it mean to live life God's way?

10. What additional thoughts or ideas from this chapter would you like to explore?

Activities

As a group: Take out the keys you are carrying with you and briefly think about what each one is for. Then, using paper and pencils or other art supplies, create a "Key to Life" use for each key. For example, "My house key opens the door to God in my life," "My car key reminds me that God travels with me," and so on. Share the meaning of your keys with the rest of the group.

At home: Reflect on how much you rely on God. Is God your co-pilot or your pilot? How often do you consult with God and ask for directions and guidance?

Prayer: *Dear God, thank you for always being there to guide me, protect me, and love me. I ask you to be the pilot of my life so my thoughts, words, and deeds may be pleasing to you. Amen.*

CHAPTER 2
The Priority of God

Snapshot Summary
This chapter reminds us how God empowers us to forgive, to love unconditionally, and to build a church.

Reflection/Discussion Questions
1. Share a time when God provided you with the strength you needed.
2. We are God's priority. Reflect on/ discuss how we can make God our priority.
3. Why is it important to be able to forgive others? Name some benefits of living a life of forgiveness.
4. What is the connection between forgiveness and the Holy Spirit?
5. What does it mean to love unconditionally? Give an example.
6. Name some simple ways to show the love of God to others.
7. What does James Moore mean by the statement, "Only the Holy Spirit of God can build a church"?
8. What is our calling as a church? Describe some of the opportunities and responsibilities.
9. What does it mean to you personally to be empowered by God and the Holy Spirit?

10. What additional thoughts or ideas from this chapter would you like to explore?

Activities
As a group: Use Bibles to identify priorities of believers and disciples in the New Testament. Create a group list of these priorities, such as prayer, love, and so on.
At home: Examine your priorities and think about how they match the priorities of God. Identify areas for improvement and take action to be a more effective Christian.

Prayer: *Dear God, thank you for making each of us a priority. Help us be better at loving and forgiving while ministering to others through your church. Pilot our lives and direct us to those in need. Amen.*

CHAPTER 3

The Priority of God's Three Ways of Acting

Snapshot Summary
This chapter looks into the doctrine of the Trinity and the three ways we as Christians experience and sing praise to God: as the Father-Creator, the Son-Savior, and the Holy Spirit-Sustainer.

Reflection/Discussion Questions

1. Name some things in life that are hard to define or explain.

2. Why is the concept of "one God in three persons" confusing to some people?

3. According to James Moore, what is the key to unlocking the "theological puzzle" of the Trinity?

4. How is the doctrine of the Trinity like the concept of love? What similarities do they share?

5. How have you experienced God as Father-Creator?

6. Reflect on/discuss what it means that "order implies mind."

7. In what ways does Jesus paint for us a portrait of God?

8. Reflect on/discuss James Moore's statement that if you don't have Jesus in your heart, your life will be an empty shell.

9. Name some of the different ways in which God sustains us.

10. What additional thoughts or ideas from this chapter would you like to explore?

Activities

As a group: Use hymnals to locate words and phrases that relate to or describe the Holy Trinity. Create a group list of these words.

At home: Reflect upon your reading and discussion of this chapter to gain new insights into the Holy Trinity.

Prayer: *Dear God, thank you for making us, for saving us, and for sustaining us. You are an amazing and awesome God. Continue to pilot each of us through this journey, and help us grow closer to you and to others. Amen.*

CHAPTER 4
The Priority of the Prince of Peace

Snapshot Summary
This chapter explores issues relating to war and peace. It reminds us that our world has become a global village, that there are similarities among all people of this world, and that Jesus Christ is the Prince of Peace.

Reflection/Discussion Questions
1. Share a wartime image or memory that had a significant impact on you.

2. What are some of the pros and cons to the "Holy War" approach to war?

3. Explain what a pacifist believes and what issues pacifists wrestle with.

4. What is the basic premise of the "Just War" approach? How is it related to what is referred to as "Humane Fighting"?

164

5. Talk about the advantages and disadvantages of the "Waging War by Sanctions" approach.

6. With acknowledgment that there may be respectful disagreement, share your opinion on which of the four approaches to war has the most merit.

7. In what ways has our world become a global village? Describe some of the implications.

8. Name some similarities that all the people of the world share.

9. What lessons about God and peace can be learned from Jesus' encounter with the disturbed man in Mark 5?

10. What additional thoughts and ideas from this chapter would you like to explore?

Activities

As a group: Create a list of what Christians can do to work for world peace.

At home: Look for opportunities to become a peacemaker at home, at work, or in your community this week.

Prayer: *Dear God, thank you for reminding us of the importance of peace and how each of us can make a difference. Help us remember that Jesus is our Prince of Peace and that he is our best hope for a peaceful world. Amen.*

CHAPTER 5
The Priority of Christlikeness

Snapshot Summary
This chapter focuses on the prayers that Jesus prayed while on the cross. These prayers show what it means to be Christlike.

Reflection/Discussion Questions
1. Why are the seven last words or statements of Christ so powerful and memorable?

2. What do the cross prayers have in common? How are they different?

3. What thoughts and feelings does Jesus reveal by praying for his executioners?

4. What can we learn about forgiveness and unconditional love from Jesus' words on the cross?

5. List and discuss the three classic interpretations, as James Moore outlines them, of Jesus' statement, "My God, why hast thou forsaken me?"

6. Share a time when you felt forsaken. What does that feel like?

7. Reflect on/discuss what is known about the prayer, "Father, into Thy hands I commend my spirit."

8. How do you begin to make Christlikeness a priority in your life?

166

9. What do all the words from the cross reveal about Jesus?

10. What additional thoughts or ideas from this chapter would you like to explore?

Activities

As a group: Let each member of the group write a brief prayer that reflects thoughts or ideas from this chapter. Collect your prayers and use them as your group's closing prayer. *At home:* Reflect upon what it means to be Christlike. Read the passages from the Bible concerning Jesus' death on the cross.

Prayer: *Dear God, thank you for the moving prayers of Jesus upon the cross. Help us remember the love and sacrifice of our Lord. Amen.*

CHAPTER 6
The Priority of the Holy Spirit

Snapshot Summary

This chapter explores Pentecost and the three traditional symbols of the Holy Spirit in the Bible — breath, fire, and the descending dove.

Reflection/Discussion Questions

1. When you think of Pentecost, what images come to mind?

2. As the disciples waited for the arrival of the Holy Spirit, what do you think were their thoughts and feelings?

3. Describe the arrival of the Holy Spirit as experienced by the disciples.

4. Reflect on/discuss what it means that "God works from the inside out."

5. What does breath represent as a symbol for the Holy Spirit?

6. How and why have some people blocked the Holy Spirit from their lives?

7. Talk about the firepower of Pentecost and what it enables us to do.

8. What does the descending dove represent?

9. How do you know the Holy Spirit is within you?

10. What additional thoughts or ideas from this chapter would you like to explore?

Activities

As a group: Imagine that you and your small group are the disciples of Jesus, waiting for the Holy Spirit to arrive. Let each group member write down what he or she is feeling and experiencing as you wait. Share what you have written with the rest of the group.

At home: Reflect on the meaning of Pentecost and why it is important to you.

Prayer: *Dear God, thank you for the gift of the Holy Spirit and Pentecost. Help us give the Holy Spirit more room to operate within us and guide us in doing your will. Amen.*

CHAPTER 7

The Priority of Gratitude to God

Snapshot Summary
This chapter examines the choices we face in every situation: we can encourage or discourage, laugh or lament, and celebrate or complain.

Reflection/Discussion Questions
1. What impressed you about the story of the pilgrims?

2. Share a time when you were grateful to God. What words and feelings would you use to describe your mood?

3. What lessons can we learn from the story of Jesus and the ten men with leprosy?

4. Share a time when you were faced with the choice to encourage or discourage.

5. Reflect on/discuss the importance of

laughter and having a good sense of humor.

6. Give some reasons why people complain. Does it do any good to complain? Why or why not?

7. Reflect on/discuss why it is important to celebrate small victories and accomplishments.

8. Brainstorm ways to develop the habit of gratitude.

9. When faced with the choices described in this chapter, what sorts of things might you do to ensure that you make the right choice?

10. What additional thoughts or ideas from this chapter would you like to explore?

Activities

As a group: Let each group member make a list of all the choices he or she has made so far today. Compare your lists and identify the most unusual choices.

At home: Consider how you have been blessed by God. Be grateful.

Prayer: *Dear God, thank you for the countless blessings we have been given. Help us be a blessing to others and make gratitude a priority in our lives. Amen.*

CHAPTER 8

The Priority of Service to God

Snapshot Summary

This chapter reminds us of our privilege to serve God and how our service is a symbol of our gratitude, our love, and our commitment.

Reflection/Discussion Questions

1. Share a time when you came running because there was an urgent job to be done.

2. Name some of the ways God calls us to service.

3. Why is *availability* more important to God than *ability?*

4. Name some common excuses people give to avoid service to God and others.

5. How is service a symbol of our gratitude to God?

6. "We are called to be servants of love." What does this mean to you personally?

7. Talk about ways in which we can make service to God a priority.

8. What is the relationship between service and commitment?

9. Name some tasks that most every church has available to willing members who want to serve.

10. What additional thought or ideas from this chapter would you like to explore?

Activities
As a group: Create your own Full Service Pledge to serve God and others. Share your pledges.

At home: Prayerfully consider opportunities to serve God at home, at work, at church, and within the community. Take steps this week toward making service a priority.

Prayer: *Dear God, thank you for allowing us to serve you. Help us make service to you a priority, and help us listen and respond to your call. May we remember the needs of others and use our time and talents to serve those in need. Amen.*

CHAPTER 9
The Priority of God's Church

Snapshot Summary
This chapter explores the benefits of worship at church, including a right relationship with God, a right respect for other people, and a right reason for living.

Reflection/Discussion Questions

1. Drawing upon your own experience, name some of the benefits of regular church attendance.

2. Talk about the obligation and commitment made when joining a church.

3. Explain why attending church regularly is a habit, just as not going to church is also a habit.

4. When a person becomes a Christian, what promises are made to God?

5. Share your own definition of what it means to be *faithful.*

6. Discuss what it means to have a right relationship with God.

7. Explain how regular church attendance increases respect for others.

8. How does the church call members to ministry?

9. Why is it wrong to think that the work of ministry belongs only to clergy and church staff?

10. What additional thoughts or ideas from this chapter would you like to explore?

Activities

As a group: Search the Bible and make a list of the commitments God has made to all believers.

At home: Examine your commitment to

God and to the church. Is God's church a priority in your life?

Prayer: *Dear God, thank you for reminding us of the importance and benefits of regular church attendance. Help us honor the commitments we make in life to you and to others. Amen.*

CHAPTER 10

The Priority of Being a Miracle Worker for God

Snapshot Summary
This chapter shows us how, with the help of God, we can be miracle workers with our words, our attitudes, and our actions.

Reflection/Discussion Questions
1. Share a time when you experienced a love miracle.

2. Name some of the love miracles found in the Bible.

3. Give your own definition of a miracle.

4. If you had the power to perform one miracle, what would it be?

5. List some ways we can work miracles using just our words.

6. Name some of the most powerful words you know.

7. Reflect on/discuss the power of attitudes and how they can trigger miracles.

8. Name some actions that speak louder than words.

9. Reflect on/discuss how and why miracles happen when we live in the spirit of Christ.

10. What additional thoughts or ideas from this chapter would you like to explore?

Activities

As a group: Create a list naming all of the ingredients of a miracle.

At home: Look for an opportunity this week to perform a miracle.

Prayer: *Dear God, thank you for giving us the power and responsibility to become miracle workers. Open our eyes to opportunities to minister to others and to change lives. Help us reflect your love in our words and actions. Amen.*

CHAPTER 11

The Priority of Having a Strong Case of the "Can't Help It"s

Snapshot Summary

This chapter reminds us that because we are Christians, we can't help being grateful, confident, and loving.

Reflection/Discussion Questions

1. Talk about what happened to Andrew and how he felt after he found Jesus.

2. What causes people to develop a case of the "can't help it"s?

3. Share a time when you were incredibly grateful to God.

4. Reflect on/discuss the power of responsive gratitude.

5. Name some of the ways we show gratitude to God, then name some ways we show gratitude to others.

6. Share your own definition of *confidence*, and give an example of it.

7. Name some reasons why Christians can be so confident.

8. Why is the disciple Andrew a great example of love?

9. Give some reasons why Christians can't help loving others.

10. What additional thoughts or ideas from this chapter would you like to explore?

Activities

As a group: Reread Psalm 100 and search the Bible for other psalms that reverberate with gratitude.

At home: Look for an opportunity to go "out

176

of control" with gratefulness, confidence, or love this week.

Prayer: *Dear God, thank you for reminding us of the reasons we can be grateful, confident, and loving. Help us step out in faith to share your good news with others. Amen.*

CHAPTER 12
The Priority of Prioritizing

Snapshot Summary
This chapter looks at things we would do well to cut out of our lives and throw away. These include selfishness, defeat, and ill will.

Reflection/Discussion Questions
1. Name some times in life when a clean sweep is in order.
2. What did Jesus mean in Matthew 5 when he said to cut off your right hand and throw it away if it causes you to sin?
3. Give some practical applications of this "cut it off and throw it away" principle.
4. Reflect on/discuss why selfishness is so dangerous and needs to be thrown out.
5. Name some cures for selfishness.
6. What does it mean to throw out defeat? How can this be accomplished?

7. Share a time when you battled against defeat.

8. What does the phrase "ill will" mean; what sorts of things does it include?

9. How do you change "ill will" to "good-will"?

10. What additional thoughts or ideas from this chapter would you like to explore?

Activities

As a group: Create your own personal list of new priorities based on insights from your reading and discussion of this book. Share your lists.

At home: Reflect on your experience of reading and discussing this book, how it has changed you, and how you plan to make God the pilot of your life.

Prayer: *Dear God, thank you for allowing us to learn more about you and about ourselves. Help us begin a clean sweep in our lives, and help us make you the number-one priority, always. Amen.*